Take Back Your Wedding

WILLIAM J. DOHERTY, PH.D.,
ELIZABETH DOHERTY THOMAS

TAKE BACK YOUR WEDDING

MANAGING THE PEOPLE STRESS OF WEDDING PLANNING

2007

Take Back Your Wedding

TABLE OF CONTENTS

Section Four: It All Comes Together

CHAPTER ONE

TAKE BACK YOUR WEDDING

Planning a wedding is one of the hardest things you will do in your life, and one of the most thrilling when it all comes together. The hardest part is not what you might think when you get engaged—dealing with all the logistics. The hardest part is dealing with the people. Here is a typical chat room post from a disillusioned bride-to-be:

> I am seriously dreading my upcoming wedding, only because I have changed all my pre-wedding plans to accommodate others. None of my attendants make an effort to call to chat, (we live in different states), I have felt pressure to invite people I don't want there (from both families), and I now have three flower girls, one of which I don't really want in the wedding. I know I am just whining but I wonder if any of you scrapped the plans and are going to elope.

This bride's regrets prompted immediate responses in kind. Here were the first two:

> I think we've all WANTED to scrap it and elope! Planning a wedding is stressful and annoying, mostly because of everyone's "opinion" and dealing with TWO families! I think you should go along with your plans and

make sure your wedding is what YOU wanted, not what everyone else wants. You only get one day, enjoy it. I'm just beginning to plan my wedding and I've already had requests as to what date works best for THEM! Ugh!

Ha-ha, the same with me. I would have to say my mom and I are becoming real nasty to each other even though we don't mean it intentionally. My dad mentioned us eloping, but I think that made my fiancé a little upset because he thought my dad was just trying to be cheap. We're Hispanic and so automatically that means it's gonna be a big wedding, so the planning part is just beyond overwhelming....

Most weddings come off beautifully despite these hassles, and most couples are glad they did not elope. But too many brides and grooms feel like they have gone through hell getting to their wedding day. Shelves of books offer suggestions on everything from invitations to toasts, but any married couple will tell you that dealing with family members, wedding parties, and friends is the most challenging part of planning a wedding. Brides don't lose sleep over floral arrangements but over conflicts with their mothers about floral arrangements. Grooms get flummoxed not over the guest list but over their bride's insistence that they tell their parents to pare down a bloated guest list.

We are reminded of something a mayor of a large city said when a critic complained that the streets of the city were dangerous. The mayor shot back: "There's nothing dangerous about the streets in this city. It's the people...." The same could be said about weddings: there is nothing that can't be planned and carried off well—if only the people pull together. If they don't, the path towards the altar is a minefield. We wrote this book to help you avoid minefields and to walk safely through ones you can't avoid.

SO MANY DECISIONS, SO MANY PEOPLE

With the possible exception of building a house together, there is nothing in a couple's life that involves more decisions, small and large, than a wedding. All of these decisions are interconnected, with the first decisions, sometimes easy to make, producing headaches later. For example, your favorite place for a reception is miraculously free, so you book it—only to learn later that the church your favorite clergyperson has moved to is 35 miles away and the reception hall will not accommodate the number of family friends your in-laws want to invite.

Each decision in planning a wedding has stakeholders other than the bride and groom; in other words, lots of important people have strong feelings about nearly every aspect of your wedding. They care not only about what is decided but also about how they were involved in the decision. Sometimes they care deeply that someone else, like an ex-spouse, be kept out of the decision making.

Even if you are paying for the wedding yourselves, relatives and friends will have their opinions, feelings, and maybe rivalries. But if parents are footing the bill, their stake is higher and the negotiations even trickier. In fact, it may only be the honeymoon that couples choose more or less on their own, with other people mostly staying out of the decision—unless, of course, someone else is footing the bill.

All of this is complicated even if both of you come from intact two parent families, because weddings bring together two different families and their networks of friends. The complexities are magnified in post-divorce families, where four families may come together to re-enact old dramas of power and control. The bride and groom can be caught up in loyalty struggles over everything from the names on wedding invitations to toasts at the reception. On the positive side, dealing well with these complex family relationships during the wedding planning can set the stage for healthier future relationships with family members. This book will help you achieve that goal.

Then there is your own relationship as a couple. How are you going to manage the decisions and the people as you plan your wedding? Announcing your engagement is really the beginning of your marriage, because from that moment on you have serious decisions to make—and you now have in-laws. In making wedding decisions, you will have to figure out what kind of team you want to be, which tasks you will share and which you will handle separately. Before you can deal well with family and friends, you must have your own act together. As we will discuss later, no matter how you divide up responsibilities—whether traditionally or in your own unique way—each of you will have to take the lead with your own family. A particularly bad way to start a marriage is to expect the bride to handle the difficult conversations with the groom's family, or vice versa.

WHOSE WEDDING IS IT?

Elizabeth enjoyed wedding chat rooms during her engagement, finding them a source of moral support and good ideas. But she saw one form of bad advice repeated over and over to couples who were struggling with family and friends over decisions on everything from guest lists to the timing and location of the wedding: IT'S YOUR WEDDING, SO DO WHAT YOU WANT. This advice, shared as a form of common sense, was even stronger if the couple was paying for that part of the wedding.

So what's wrong with having it your own way if it's your wedding? The problem is that weddings are as much about community as about the couple. They have been that way in every culture throughout human history. If you don't want your wedding to be about your community of family and friends, then elope and have the justice of the peace's spouse be your witness. (You will just have to deal with your family and community later.) If you want to have a wedding and not just a legal ceremony, then it can't be just about you and your own preferences. It can be hard to see in the midst of negotiations with the caterer over the corking fee for the wine, but weddings are the beginning of life long bonds with a new, extended family. Not just the wedding day itself when the new clan is assembled—every stage of the planning forges a new family and community, for better or worse.

Guest lists, for example, are not just about the bride and groom's fantasy of an ideal size for a wedding, but also about both families reaching out to their networks of kin and friends, bringing them into the inner circle. Suppose one of your fathers owns a small business, considers his employees part of his "family," and wants to invite them to the wedding. You don't know most of them and don't relish having "strangers" at your wedding. However you resolve this matter (it involves money and space in addition to sentiment and loyalty), our point is that a bad way to settle it is by saying, "IT'S OUR WEDDING, SO WE WILL DO WHAT WE WANT."

Rejecting the "it's just for us" myth does not mean adopting the reverse: "Just go along and keep everyone happy." Since you are the ones getting married, you are the principal stakeholders if not the only ones. You don't have to let your mother make your wedding the one she had hoped for herself but was denied by her own mother. Your father, who likes to stress his power over the checkbook, should not have unilateral veto power. No parent should get away with manipulations to keep an ex-spouse out of the limelight. Your aunt Sophie may think that she can bake the best wedding cake in the state, but that does not equate to a decision that she will make your cake.

Doing it your way or their way may appear to be the easier paths because you don't have to deal directly with differences. But you miss the opportunity to start a new life together by working on the challenges in front of you with the people who will be in your life until theirs or your dying breaths. So we propose a different wedding motto: IT'S OUR WEDDING AND YOU'RE AN IMPORTANT PART OF IT, SO LET'S FIGURE IT OUT TOGETHER.

WHAT THIS BOOK CAN DO FOR YOU

We want this book to help you make planning your wedding a satisfying journey rather than an obstacle course, a path with challenges to be mastered rather than a mine field. We will teach you about five key steps to deal with each other as a couple and with other people involved in the wedding:

- Clarify expectations
- Negotiate differences up front
- Look deeper, when necessary, into what is behind disagreements
- Make a decision that has integrity
- Then do the work and enjoy the wedding

Some of the help we offer will be practical. For example, we will show you a process for getting everyone's expectations out on the table as soon as possible, because the first decisions you make affect later decisions. When expectations line up, or when minor differences are easily handled, so much the better. The hard work begins when expectations differ more strongly and people dig in or won't communicate. We will help you get below the surface of what is going on with your family, in-laws, wedding party, and friends when they (or you) seem stubborn, selfish, or controlling. People who care about you become obstacles to the wedding when personal feelings and relationships are on the line. It's important to understand when the paper the invitations are printed on is not the real issue in the argument, but when something else is going on. To repeat: clarifying what everyone wants and needs from their own perspective is the crucial first step in planning a wedding. It's not the logistics that make or break the wedding; it's the people.

The book will help you negotiate and make decisions in good faith and for the common good of all involved. We will give you principles that cut across different problem areas, such as the idea that the blood (or adoptive) relative should do the heavy lifting with his or her own family. Easy to say, but what if your fiancé(e) hates conflict and does not sign up for the job? We have ideas for you!

Then there are the really dicey situations that many couples face. If one or both of you come from a family of divorce, we will offer a roadmap for avoiding predictable obstacles and managing the ones you cannot avoid. Sometimes you have to be the only adult in the situation when your parents can't handle their own feelings. We will show you how to do this with integrity and respect.

You may find that a relative (or friend) is just impossible to deal with constructively after you have used all of your own resources of understanding and negotiating in good faith.

Most relatives can overcome their own insecurities and self-absorption and rise to the occasion for a family wedding. But others cannot. We will discuss strategies to prevent these people from hijacking your wedding either by controlling a key part of the wedding or rendering you emotionally preoccupied with them rather than with each other and your wedding.

WHO WE ARE AND WHY WE WROTE THIS BOOK

We are an unusual writing team. Elizabeth Doherty Thomas married her husband Michael Thomas on October 4, 2003 at ages 27 and 26, respectively. They had the normal worries and hassles in planning their wedding but relished the process and now want to pass on what they learned to other couples. Mike was involved as an active partner at every stage, in contrast to the traditional groom role. He particularly dislikes the "groom as furniture" stereotype. Elizabeth stayed in touch with many other brides through conversations and Internet chat rooms, which gave her insight into the challenges faced by contemporary engaged couples. As a young married woman (and mother), but close enough to the wedding experience, she has a unique perspective on what is most important about planning a wedding.

Bill Doherty relished being the father of the bride. He brings his experience as academic family social scientist, marriage and family therapist, and author of others books for families. Having experienced and witnessed what his family learned from putting on a wedding, he proposed this book project to Elizabeth, who jumped at the idea of writing a different kind of wedding book, one that focused on the people part rather than the task part.

This book is a collective work. We combined our ideas for each chapter, frequently consulting with our spouses. Bill wrote the first drafts, and then we massaged them until we were both satisfied. Neither of us could have written it alone. We decided to focus on weddings we know best—a bride and groom planning a "community" wedding and starting a first marriage—while acknowledging that there are many different kinds of couples, some with kids already, and other more private weddings. Couples in other situations, however, may benefit from the central ideas in the books.

If the first bit of bad advice for engaged couples is to do your own thing and not worry about what others want, a second kind of unwise advice can come from experienced married couples: don't worry so much about the wedding because it's the marriage itself that counts. Our view is different: planning your wedding is the beginning of your marriage relationship. We urge you to use this time to access the wealth of educational programs available nowadays. Our website www.TheFirstDance.com has a list of resources you can consult to find local premarital education programs, including www.smartmarriages.com and www.healthymarriageinfo.org. In fact, the issues we raise in this book would be ideal fodder for trying out the knowledge and communications skills you can learn in a good premarital education program. Our website also describes an educational DVD based on this book, along with our wedding stress coaching service for couples who want personal help via telephone or instant messaging.

Although we all know that marriage is a life long project, for now you are building your marriage mostly by planning your wedding together. How you communicate now will stay with you, as will how you deal with your differences. How you support each other now with the stresses of the wedding will lay down the template for your future, as will how you deal with your families. You are preparing for the biggest event of your lives, the birth of your marriage in the embrace of your community. We are thrilled that you have taken our book on your journey. If you have stories to pass on, or feedback about our book, we would love to hear from you at our email address: feedback@thefirstdance.com.

CHAPTER TWO

GUESS WHAT? YOU'RE MARRYING YOUR IN-LAWS!

Announce your engagement and you immediately become an in-law. Like it or not, you join a new family. This truth, well known to every married couple on the planet, somehow hits every newly engaged couple like a meteorite striking from the sky. You not only have your own (lovable but sometimes difficult) family to deal with, but you now have this other family, with their strange ways and demanding cast of characters. And these two families of strangers somehow have to work together to plan a wedding. It's dealing with the families that brings many brides and grooms to their knees. Here is a colorful example from a chat room for brides:

> I have nearly killed every member of my own and my fiancé's families so far.... We have 8 hellish months to go and I am HATING all this planning. Nobody likes anything I have already chosen, am going to do, or will get around to doing.... AND IT'S MY DAY! My fiancé, one night when I was screaming hysterically and crying all over him saying how much I hated everything that was happening around me, said "Screw it, let's cancel it all and go to Jamaica!" At first I said yes, then I realized he intended to STILL have both our families there so I figured, why do it? THESE ARE THE VERY PEOPLE

I WANT TO KILL! So, I would merely be moving my hell from one place to another. Great. We are still having the wedding we originally planned, but I swear I wish I had just gone down the local registry office with my fiancé and said "Marry us now, please!" and then told our families to get over it!!!! Urgh :(

Okay, so maybe this bride is a bit extreme, but she is expressing common bewilderment, frustration, and despair. Can you see her first mistake? It's her assumption that the decisions are hers alone and that her family and in-laws should simply line up in support: "Nobody likes anything I have already chosen, am going to do, or will get around to doing.... AND IT'S MY DAY!"

Here is a big, if painful, lesson: *It's not just your day.* Even if you find a Justice of the Peace in Jamaica and ask a beach bum to be your witnesses, you still are officially joining each other's families on that day. Relatives will have strong feelings about not being invited. They will still buy you gifts and probably still hold a party for you. (Your own kids some day will learn your story and maybe exclude you from their own weddings.) Weddings are a big a deal for nearly every family. You will not be able to dismiss their support when they like what you are doing or their disapproval when they don't. Marry each other and you are marrying each other's families: it's a package deal. On your wedding day, you will be the lead actors in the drama, the center of everyone's attention, but there will be lots of others on stage and behind the scenes.

It's too bad we don't start becoming in-laws during the more carefree dating period when the biggest decisions are where to have dinner and which set of friends to hang out with. Parents usually leave courting couples alone to explore their relationship; family contact is usually casual and free of serious conflict unless the parents actively dislike the girlfriend or boyfriend. Even if you were living together before the engagement, you were not yet someone's in-law. But engagement brings a double whammy: you join each other's families and at that very instant you begin one of the most difficult planning tasks in modern life. There is no easing into it: "We're engaged, welcome to the family, and how in the world are we going to pull off this wedding?"

GETTING TO KNOW YOU, GETTING TO KNOW ALL ABOUT YOU

You don't really know someone until you have to make decisions with him or her. Many engaged couples are blindsided when formerly friendly, laid-back parents suddenly become controlling, critical, picky, or irrational. We'd like to help you understand what might be going on. The wedding of a child brings forth feelings and reactions from parents that can make sense to you if you stop and reflect—something hard to do because you are caught up in your own feelings. But if you can put aside your own perspective and try to understand your parents, it can make your wedding planning a lot easier on yourselves. Here are common reactions parents have to their child's wedding:

- *Joy and Pride.* It's a parent's dream that their child will find someone to marry and spend their life with. These are the feelings you expect them to have, but these feelings are sometimes less visible than the next ones once you get into the wedding planning.
- *Loss.* Getting married means starting a new family, which means leaving your parents. This is true even if you moved out a decade ago; they still feel responsible for you if your life hits the skids. When you marry,

your spouse is more responsible for the child that your parents have raised and protected. The sense of loss can be quite acute when there has been an especially intense bond with one of the parents.

- *Anxiety.* This can come in many forms: worry about your future marriage, concern about how extended family or ex-spouses will behave, frets about expenses, and a general nervousness about planning a wedding and about what other people will think of the job they do.

- *Envy.* When parents have regrets about their own marriages and divorces, they may envy the happiness of their child, the relationship they have with their fiancé, and the fresh start they have in life. Rarely will they tell you this directly.

- *Competition.* When two families come together to plan a wedding, they bring different resources, communities, and expertise. You can be sure your parents will pay attention to which family has more money and status. Sometimes decisions are driven by not wanting to lose face with the other family.

When both sets of parents are having these feelings at the same time that you and your fiancé are caught up in your own intense feelings—well, it's a volatile brew. (At wedding rehearsals, a minister friend of ours often looks for an extended family member, such as an aunt, who might be the only person in the room who has perspective on things.) Understanding what is going on beneath the surface in yourself and your parents can help you make sense out of situations such as the following one involving Sara and her mom. Sara's mom had been divorced for many years, but had known Sara's fiancé, Joe, for a decade, since the time the couple were high school sweethearts. Joe was practically family, went to all the family reunions, and helped himself in Mom's kitchen when he came over. So when Sara and Joe got engaged, Sara was shocked by her mom's sudden shift in attitude. Her mom was sad, snippy about "too much wedding talk," and not cooperative in wedding discussions. She also made critical comments about Joe and his family that seemed completely out of character for her.

Sara brought this up in the couple's premarital counseling, and the counselor helped her understand the probable source of her mother's strange reaction. After so many years of a tight mother-daughter relationship in a single parent family, Mom was losing her friend and confidante. She was probably also re-living her divorce, and perhaps worrying about whether her daughter's marriage would also end up in divorce. There was no way to be sure about these explanations, because Mom was not being open about her feelings, but the conversation with the counselor helped Sara feel compassion for her mother instead of just surprise and annoyance. Equally important, Sara came to understand that she could not fix her mother's feelings and take away her fears. For his part, Joe found that he could now take his future mother-in-law's criticisms less personally. Eventually Mom got more into the joy and pride parts of her reactions, and the wedding process improved. But it could have been awful.

Sometimes the problem is that one set of parents is not very reliable, something their child knows but not the fiancé. Carol and Steve had very little money to pay towards the wedding, but fortunately his parents said they were willing to put a good amount down for the wedding. But as the wedding planning progressed, things got more and more sticky as his parents started backpedaling on how much they wanted to spend. What really frustrated Carol was that these same people, who said they didn't have the $2,000 deposit to put down on the reception hall, proceeded to spend $5,000 towards remodeling their summer cabin. How could they do this to her and her wedding? Why wasn't Steve sticking up for their wedding plans with his parents?

It turned out that Steve was never confident that his parents would follow through. They had bad spending habits that included wishful thinking and impulsive purchases. Because of his embarrassment, he did not let Carol in on this family secret until after the fact. In a later chapter we will talk about how to deal with this kind of conflict. For here we note that it was important for Carol and Steve to realize that his parents could not be relied upon for straight communication about money, and for them to plan accordingly. Carol in particular could either torture herself, and her fiancé, over the kind of family she was marrying into, or she could take to heart this lesson: *Difficult in-laws are like dealing with the weather: you hope for the best, forget about changing them, do damage control when necessary, and keep moving ahead.*

CLASH OF FAMILY WEDDING TRADITIONS

Because Stephanie's parents had real money, Brian envisioned the ritzy wedding he'd secretly always wanted but knew his parents could never have afforded for his sister. Finally, he was going to be able to ride in a limo, own expensive kitchenware (he was an aspiring chef), and go on a fantastic honeymoon, all without much effort from Stephanie's rich parents. He didn't want to sound greedy so he laid low in talking about the wedding with Stephanie, until Stephanie's parents sat them down one day and spelled out the money they were willing to spend—less than half of what it would cost for a decent wedding! Brian was angry. Later he started complaining to Stephanie about how greedy her parents were, and how obnoxious it was that they were buying a new expensive home and new furniture for their 3rd home, but weren't going to pay for whole wedding. Stephanie was shocked at Brian's reaction. It turns out that she never thought her parents would pay for the wedding at all, because that was not part of the family tradition and in fact she was tired of feeling "used" by their money. Finally she was going to set herself free as an adult with minimal money (and therefore fewer power struggles) with her parents. She started questioning if she wanted to marry this greedy man! What we have here is a difference in family cultures or traditions, not a greedy groom and miserly parents. Understanding their families could have helped this couple understand each other.

Things get particularly tricky when both families are involved in the decision making. Jess and Mitch talked with her parents and his parents about helping pay for the wedding. His parents had more money, but her parents had a sense of pride about paying for their daughters wedding. Unfortunately, the amount they were able to spend was so small it would barely feed fifty wedding guests, let alone the reception, wedding dress, flowers, limo, and so on. Mitch knew his parents would help out without question, so when he approached Jess's parents, he was not prepared for their negative reaction and hurt feelings. What was the big deal? Mitch wondered. Of course, one big mistake was for Mitch to approach his in-laws on his own, failing to heed the next lesson: *Blood talks to blood; each partner carries the main responsibility for difficult family conversations.*

Beyond this strategic blunder, Mitch did not appreciate the importance of family pride and face saving over a wedding. These are delicate negotiations that the blood relative is best positioned to carry out. In Jess and Mitch's case, she was able to put the issue to her parents in a way they could accept by emphasizing that she was grateful for their generous support for the wedding and that Mitch's parents were also eager to help the bride and groom. It would feel so good to have both families contributing, she stressed. Her parents went along for the sake of their daughter's wishes, an easier pill to swallow than having their future son-in-law say bluntly that his parents had plenty of money they were willing contribute to the wedding.

There are lots of family differences besides money ones. Here are some that come up frequently around wedding planning:

- *Casual versus Formal.* In one case, the bride's "trailer trash" family (her own term) could not imagine anything but a formal wedding because of their tradition. The groom's middle class family was the more casual one, and was less comfortable with a high church wedding and ballroom reception. The groom joined his family in mocking his in-laws, who already felt inferior to his family.
- *Showy versus Shy.* Some families are naturally outgoing in public, patting every back in sight, while others are more reserved until they get to know people. The movie "Meet the Fockers" hilariously shows the results when the two family cultures collide without understanding their differences.
- *Tons of Friends versus a Small Circle.* When some parents say they want to invite their close friends, it's a hundred or more. For others, it's their five friends from elementary school.
- *Pushy versus Evasive.* Some parents will give you advice you never asked for and wonder why you have not taken it, while others won't tell you what they are thinking lest they infringe on your decision making or feel responsible for a mistake.

The key to working with these differences between families is to understand and accept them as neither good nor bad, but just the way your families are. There are always advantages and disadvantages no matter what. But it's hard to see this because we grow up in one family with its own slant on being a family. If your parents are pushy, this feels like how parents should be, even if they are annoying at times. Casual seems like a law of nature, not just one way of being in the world. The most important thing is not let these differences come between you and your fiancé, which means avoiding direct criticism of your in-laws' family style. It will only make your partner defensive and invite a counterattack on your family. Therefore, the next lesson is crucial, worth remembering all your life: *Thou shalt not mock the ways of your in-laws, strange though they may be.*

Beyond family differences in style and temperament lie thorny areas such as race, religion, and regional culture. These differences individually can make the other family seem strange indeed. When you combine them, the families can seem like they come from different planets. Picture an evangelical Southern Baptist family having a church wedding with a groom's family of North Dakota Lutherans. It's the stuff of movies. Part of the job of the bride and groom is to become like anthropologists to understand each other's family culture, and then to teach their own families about the other. Elizabeth and Mike did this with their respective upper Midwest and Southern families, helping each understand the other as we entered the wedding planning.

WHEN YOUR FAMILY IS SPLINTERED

Divorced families and stepfamilies present special challenges for couples planning a wedding. (We will return to this theme frequently in the book.) Susan and Jeff thought everything was set after her divorced parents came to an agreement on what they would contribute towards the wedding. It came to about 90 percent of the total cost for the wedding, covering everything except rings, honeymoon, and the music. Soon thereafter, Jeff got a huge promotion at work and there was a family celebration over the good news that after years of schooling and hard work, Jeff was finally in the kind of position he had worked so hard for. At this event, Susan's step-mom shockingly announced that she wanted the money Susan's dad had put down returned to him; not another penny of his should go to the wedding, she declared. Jeff was livid and a big screaming match ensued between the step-mom and Jeff. Susan wanted to crawl into a hole or run away. Fortunately, Susan's father did not go along with his wife, but the hurt feelings never fully went away.

Obviously, this was a catastrophic mistake by the stepmother. What can Susan and Jeff learn from it? Don't trust the stepmother, for one thing. But at a deeper level, Jeff needs education from Susan about the dark side of her family. People don't do what the stepmother did without a lot of family history of competition, rivalry, and feelings of being used. In fact, the biological parents usually share a big part of the responsibility when stepfamily problems break out this way. For example, it is likely that Susan's father had not made it completely clear to his second wife that Susan was a big priority to him and that he did not resent financially supporting her wedding. If instead he had complained for years about child support and college tuition, which limited his financial contributions to his new family, then the stepmother would have built up a pile of resentment about this outgoing cash from her own family. Perhaps he had told his wife that he was contributing to the wedding only because he did not want to be shown up by his ex-wife. For any number of reasons, it might have seemed to the stepmother that it was unnecessary burden on her family to pay for the wedding of a financially independent daughter who she probably did not get along with. When the stepmother heard about Jeff's big raise, years of resentment spilled out in a hostile and inappropriate way. She may have ended up being the "fall guy" for her husband, who by the way, did not silence her immediately after her outburst and let his future son-in-law argue with his wife.

This is all conjecture, of course, but it's a plausible explanation for why this woman came across like the Wicked Stepmother and caused tremendous hurt to the bride and groom. Our main point is that when you marry into a family who has faced divorce and remarriage, it's important to work on understanding the complex relationships, loyalties, and resentments so that you can avoid the minefields on the journey ahead. To repeat lesson two: In-laws are like dealing with the weather: you hope for the best, forget about changing them, do damage control when necessary, and keep moving ahead.

Getting engaged marks a new stage of your relationships with your own parents, a stage in which you and your parents will have intense, complicated feelings as well as practical, logistical concerns. It marks an end of an era when you could claim top loyalty in one another's lives (even if you did not always get along) and the beginning of one where your first loyalty is to your spouse, second to children you will have, and third to your parents. It's the way it's supposed to be, but it can be confusing and wrenching. Wedding planning is your first opportunity to carve out this new relationship with your parents. It's a coming of age for all of you.

And then there are your in-laws, now your family but forever tinged with a bit of strangeness because you did not grow up with them. You never formed the unique bond of attachment that occurs between infants and parents and then grows stronger over thousands of days and nights under the same roof. What makes in-law relationships unique is that you are both family and non-family. Even if you think your partner's parents are the coolest people on earth, and they feel the same about you, there will still be challenges ahead as you form a new family together. For most of us, though, it's not love at first sight with our in-laws. We have to work at bonding with them, at understanding them and accepting them. The biggest reason to work on being a good in-law is simple: it's important for your marriage. Nothing is harder on a new marriage than getting constant complaints about your family from your new spouse—even if you agree with most of the complaints! You don't have to love your in-laws, you don't even have to admire them and their customs. But you have to accept them and not be their main critics, for the sake of your spouse and your marriage. There is no better time to work on being a good in-law than right now while you are planning your wedding with the love of your life, who is also learning to be an in-law in your family.

CHAPTER THREE

DREAMS AND REALITIES: GETTING EVERYONE'S EXPECTATIONS ON THE TABLE

No sooner do you say, "We're engaged," then the avalanche of questions commences: where, when, how big, what kind of ceremony, who will pay for what? Will Aunt Rita be making your cake? Will Pastor Tom do the ceremony? Who will be the maid of honor? Other announcements in life are much easier; announcing you are pregnant elicits just one main question: When are you due? But with weddings, everyone in the world expects lots of answers. And they often have their own very clear ideas about what those answers should be. If you are not careful, you can get lost as a couple in the first flurry of decisions.

In this chapter we will help you get your act together before you go too far down the path with your family and friends. The first big question is so obvious that many couples skip it. It's not about location, cost, or preachers. The first big question is what kind of team you want to be as a couple in planning your wedding. How do you want to do this together? A number of ways can work as long as you are clear with each other. Here are three kinds of partnerships we have observed, arranged from more traditional to less traditional:

- The bride is in charge. The bride is the planner and decision maker. She keeps the groom informed and may assign him certain tasks.

- Leader/Supporter. The bride is the clear leader but the groom helps make decisions and may have his own areas of responsibility, such as dealing with his parents and the men in the wedding party.
- Co-Leaders: They make all major decisions together. They often divide responsibility for gathering information prior to making joint decisions, and they may also have some separate areas of responsibility.

Given that our own wedding planning experiences were closer to the "co-leaders" than the other two, we have a bias towards this kind of partnership. But as we said, any of these approaches can work as long as both people are clear and feel okay with the arrangement. Each also has its disadvantages. The co-leaders may argue more because they have to negotiate more decisions. The leader and supporter can run into problems when he feels trumped on a decision he cares a lot about, and when she feels he is not following through on his responsibilities. The fully in charge bride can feel overwhelmed by the responsibility and resentful about carrying the total load, and the groom may feel like an outsider during the planning of his own wedding.

Regardless of how you decide to divide your roles, we hold two firm convictions: both of you should express your dreams and ideals for your wedding, and each of you should take primary responsibility for dealing with your own family. Later in the book we will return to the family matters. For now we focus on how to talk openly and constructively about what you each want for your wedding.

WHAT IS YOUR IDEAL WEDDING?

Although there are hundreds of decisions in planning a wedding, there is a shorter list of key ones that reflect your cherished hopes for your wedding. We have developed a worksheet (Table 3.1) to help you clarify your expectations for six key areas of your wedding: location, size, season, ceremony, wedding party, and who will pay. All of these decisions affect one another, and there will be challenges in implementing them as a package. Being clear on what you prefer, what you feel you must have, and where you can bend, will help you avoid future conflict.

There is lots of advice available to you about the timing and logistics for deciding these matters. Our interest is on how you can surface your hopes and ideals, so that you can understand each other better and be a good working team as you begin your discussions with your families and other stakeholders in you wedding. Fill out the worksheet separately and then plan a time to discuss it after you had read the rest of this chapter, which will prepare you for the challenges you may face in the conversation.

Table 3.1
WORKSHEET
WHAT DO YOU EACH HOPE FOR IN YOUR WEDDING?

Directions: Photocopy and then complete this worksheet separately before you talk about it. It's okay if one of you does not have clear ideas about what you want; you may develop ideas after talking with your partner. Give each area a priority score to indicate how important it is to you. 1 = it's an extremely high priority, 10 = you could care less.

Location (ceremony and reception). Priority # _____
1. Do you have a definite location in mind? _____
• If yes, it is _____
• If no, do you have a general idea of where? _____

Example: Ceremony in a religious setting, outdoors, in a resort setting.

Reception in same place as above, or a restaurant, hotel, a rented hall, someone's backyard, at the beach, in a house or mansion

2. What is it about your answer above that makes you want what you want?

- Does it evoke a certain emotion? _____
    Which emotion? _____

- Is it a place you've seen a wedding take place before? _____
    If so, what appealed to you? _____

- Is it a family expectation? _____
    If yes, what do you think your family wants? _____
    _____
    What priority (1-10) do you think they give it? ____
    _____

- Do you have a personal connection (an uncle who owns the restaurant and would donate the place and food?)? _____
    If yes, what is it? _____

Guest List (ceremony and reception) Priority # _____

A way to think about size, other than "small, medium, large" is to consider the types of people you expect to be at your wedding or reception, and then attach rough numbers to these. If you each write down just your side of the guest list, you can add up the numbers to see where you're at. Mutual friends shouldn't be double counted, so mark them in a "shared" category. Elizabeth found she was more willing to exclude a category of friends, but when Mike wanted his same category to be there, she then wanted to change her own opinion!

1. Family: includes
   Immediate family _____
   Relatives _____
   Close friends who are considered family _____
2. Friends: includes categories like:
   From school (elementary up through
   graduate school) _____
   From clubs and intramural sports _____
   From work (past or present) _____
   From church _____

Season—Priority # _____
   1. I know exactly what season I want _____
   2. I know what I don't want (snow, heat, rain...) _____
   3. Is there a bad time of year for a key player?
   4. Is there a time when extended family takes a vacation and couldn't make two trips close together?
   5. If there is a lot of travel involved for people, are their cheaper times of the year (winter in Aspen being a peak expensive time to travel versus summer)

Ceremony—Priority # _____
   1. I know exactly how it will look, down to the exact officiant _____
   2. I have an opinion on whether it's religious or not_____
      I want a traditional ceremony of _____
   3. I want a non-traditional ceremony consisting of the following elements _____
   4. I want a mix of tradition and personal aspects _____

Wedding Party—Priority # _____
   1. Do you know exactly who you want?
   2. Is there anyone who is going to expect to be an attendant for the bride or grooms side because they're family or close friends?

3. Do you have concerns about the numbers? Is the ceremony location going to be an issue with a small area and nine attendants on each side

4. Rehearsal dinners usually involve the wedding party and the spouses, so make sure your numbers mesh with whoever is paying and the location of the dinner.

Who will Pay—Priority # _____

1. Do you know exactly who will pay? ____

2. Will there be strings attached? Expectations? Struggles and fights? Are they going to give the money freely in one fell swoop or expect to authorize all payments to all vendors and for all supplies?

Other Priority Areas: _____ Priority # _____

_____ Priority # _____

_____ Priority # _____

HOW BIG, HOW SMALL?

The size of the wedding is one of the main stumbling blocks for couples and families. The choice of who to include and exclude is fraught with both emotional and financial implications. It involves you as a couple and also your families and friends.

Size involves not only the big picture of what you envision as you look out over the room where you wedding is held and as you greet your guests in a receiving line or afterwards at the reception. It's also about including and excluding specific people and categories of people—that's why it's hard. And those inclusions and exclusions involve the feelings and wishes of parents or grandparents who expect to have a say. Everyone has very different notions of what is acceptable. Some brides want as many people as possible, even if they have never met a lot of people in attendance. Others cry at the thought of looking out at the pews filled with people they don't recognize. Some grooms assume that their buddies from elementary school will of course be invited, while others envision a small family wedding.

For some parents, a wedding is a time to invite everyone in their entire circle of acquaintances—such as the boss who invites a hundred employees, most of whom don't know his daughter or son. What if the other family has only a small circle of acquaintances? Or does not want to invite co-workers? All of this is complicated by the question of who is paying for which aspects of the wedding, and by whether either of you, or your families, believes in a fifty-fifty split of the guest list. Then add in divorced parents on one or both sides, each with new spouses who have friends and relatives they might want to include. It's no wonder that wedding planning often hits the rocks early on the decision of how big the guest list should be, and which kinds of people should be included and excluded.

Another tricky decision related to the wedding size is the wedding party. While some people find it very simple to pick out wedding party attendants, others struggle with all the relationships, past-behaviors of drunken attendants, family, stepsiblings, and friends. Add location to the mix—whose hometown is the wedding in?—and it can be very stressful. It's important to figure out what role you want your attendants to play; for example, if the groom has 3 sisters that expect to be in the wedding party but live 2000 miles away, while the bride expects local attendants to help with dress shopping and wedding planning, these issues can be worked out if you think through it well and find ways to avoid conflict (particularly in the family since you'll be seeing your sister-in-laws the rest of your life!)

PITFALLS TO AVOID

Let's face it: if you are a traditionally raised woman and man, the bride will have a fuller picture of her ideal wedding. If you are the bride, there is a better than even chance you have been thinking about this off and on since age six. You probably have been paying careful attention to the weddings you have attended as an adult. Too big, too small, too formal, too casual, too ostentatious, too simple, right mood, wrong mood, perfect music, distracting music—and so forth. For the groom, chances are that you did not start to pay attention to weddings until your friends began to marry, and that you do not have as many clearly formed ideals and preferences as your fiancée does. Guys generally don't ask other guys if they thought the reception centerpieces were tacky.

All of this can work to your advantage if you play it right—men can come fresher to the discussion and women can come with a longer history of observation—but your differences can also keep you from having a balanced conversation about some very important matters. Even if as a bride you are going to make most of the decisions about the wedding, you will feel better about the decisions if you know what your future husband hopes for from his wedding. If both of you are going to work closely together on the wedding, it's obviously important to get your expectations on the table early in the process.

In an unfortunately common example of misfiring, Nora told her fiancé Greg that she had always dreamed of a small, intimate wedding in the tiny chapel on the campus where they had both attended college. At the time, he could not think of a reason for her not to have her dream, so he agreed. Only after the chapel was booked did Greg tell Nora that he had "kind of hoped" to have his whole extended family come to the wedding. His clan alone would more than fill the chapel.

She flipped, and brouhaha ensued between the couple and both of their families. Greg had not been acting on bad faith; he had not made the connection between the first decision on the lovely location and the later decision on the size of the guest list. And Nora and Greg together had made the mistake of not putting all of their expectations on the table at the same time. Each part of the wedding planning affects the other, and each member of the couple may feel strongly about different decisions.

This story points to another aspect of getting clear on your expectations: often it's good to express your ideal wish but then do some homework on whether it's feasible before agreeing on it, let alone acting on it. As the groom, your dream may be a wedding in the ski resort town of Breckenridge, Colorado. You and your bride met on a ski slope and Breckenridge is your favorite getaway spot. As the bride, you are willing to consider his novel idea, but your own ideal location is your hometown in Louisiana. Before trying to come to a decision on this important matter, you should both go farther down the list of expectations and consider the season and where the guests will be traveling from. Say it's a winter wedding on the ski slope. His people are from the mountains of Utah and are used to driving in snow, while her Louisiana relatives panic when they see flurries. You have a problem, particularly if you want to invite a lot of relatives and friends. In this case, your common preference for a big wedding may need to override the innovative idea of getting married in a ski resort. On the other hand, if you both wanted a very small wedding with just a few family members, then maybe Breckenridge in winter would be your common choice—you can drive the southern relatives in from the airport—with perhaps a reception a week later in Louisiana. A wedding is like a complex organism where every part affects the other. Piecemeal decisions because one of you has a great idea can get you in trouble.

PUTTING REGIONAL DIFFERENCES ON THE TABLE

We take for granted lots of things about weddings, based on our region of the country. If you and your spouse hail from different regions, or even if you do not, you can run into difficulties later on if you do not talk about nitty-gritty matters such as wedding registries, attire, and cash bar versus open bar. People have very strong feelings about matters like this, based on what is proper and expected in their part of the world. Bridal chat rooms on the Internet are filled with queries from brides asking for help from others in different parts of the country. For example, a bride from New England wanted to know what in the world a "dollar dance" was, something she was expected to do at the reception. It seemed bizarre to her that guests would pay a dollar for the privilege of dancing with her, but her fiancé took it for granted. What's a reception without a dollar dance? In fact, the key to understanding the importance of regional, cultural, and family assumptions about weddings is knowing that everyone will ask: What's a wedding without....? The problem is that different groups have different practices without which the wedding would be a bust.

Now is the time to put all of this on the table so that you can make decisions based on good information, rather than discover later that your Georgia in-laws would be greatly offended to have to pay for the alcohol at their son's wedding reception in California, or that your Texas relatives will feel embarrassed to show up in Texas wedding attire at a black tie Boston wedding. Table 3.2 contains differences that can vary by region (as well as by individual families). It's just a starter list. You would be wise to interview people in the other clan to find out what they think is essential for a wedding to be a real wedding in their neck of the woods. Internet chat rooms can be another more objective source of information about differences across the country. Then let your friends and your side of the family know what you end up deciding.

Sometimes it's not for you to decide, but just to accept what the other family and set of friends will do anyway. In some parts of the country, people mostly give cash gifts, while in other regions that is considered lazy and insulting. Some folks consider learning about your wedding registry extremely helpful, because then they know what you would like. Other folks think it's grubby and rude. No problem either way— unless the communities of the bride and groom see things differently. Now's the time to find out.

TABLE 3.2
EXAMPLES OF REGIONAL DIFFERENCES
Gifts versus cash
Whether to do seating assignments at the reception
Cash bar versus open bar
Types of registry items (heirloom quality vs casual)
hen dinner is served at the reception (early evening versus late)
Type of attire
Reception fun (dollar dance, chicken dance, etc.)
Post-wedding bar hopping
Regional Food

TALKING TOGETHER ABOUT YOUR IDEAL
WEDDING

Before reading this section, make sure you have filled out the worksheet in Table 3.1. Make sure you each do it alone so that you think independently. In the next chapter we will talk about handling conflicts and disagreements over wedding decisions. Here we will offer some ground rules for talking in a way to put both of your expectations on the table.

1. *Read first, then talk.* Look over each of your lists before picking out a particular item to discuss. It's a mistake to pick on the first item that hits your eye because you disagree with it. The conversation will get derailed and you may not realize how much agreement you have in other areas. Respectfully go over the whole list. Get the big picture of your partner's hopes, priorities, and kind of involvement he or she hopes for in the decisions. If your partner starts talking before you have finished reading, gently ask for more time.

2. *This is time for sharing ideas and ideals, not for big decisions.* People are more open-minded when they don't feel that a big decision is pending at any moment. You may need time to investigate your options or to reflect on differences that come up in your conversation. You can remind yourselves that you are having an exploratory conversation right now, to surface your ideal fantasies, rather than locking in anything.

3. *Be open-minded and curious.* Ask your partner for details beyond a simple statement of wanting the wedding to be "fun." Have them paint a picture for you of what the ceremony or reception would look like. This may stimulate your own thinking and you could come up with a shared idea.

4. *When differences surface, note how big a priority the issue is for each of you.* This is where the "priority scale" can be helpful. The groom might have written down his

ideal location on the beach near his favorite volleyball site, while the bride favors the 200-year-old Cathedral. For him, it may be a low-priority lark of an idea to get married on the beach. He may decide to drop it when he learns that hers is a number one priority on her list.

5. *Even if you agree on something, make the decision tentative.* As we said before, wedding decisions interlock in complex ways. It's best to make sure you understand all the implications before you make a decision final. If you lock in on the reception hall before learning that you will have to use a church 45 miles away (because your first choice in churches was booked), you will have created complications for yourselves that you might have avoided. Sometimes you should talk to your families first, because their input is essential.

6. *Make sure the groom gets a lot of airtime in the conversation.* We want to avoid stereotypes here, but what if the groom does not have much to say about his ideals for the wedding? What if he wants to defer to his bride about all the decisions? Our answer: don't let him off the hook. Every man (and woman) we know has opinions and hopes for their wedding, but some have trouble articulating these opinions and hopes. Sometimes it's just knowing what they *don't* want, such as a stiff country club reception or a hoedown in a barn. For each item on the list you discuss, it might be best for the groom to go first in sharing what he has written down and what his priorities are. The bride might ask for elaboration ("tell me more," "give me a for instance") before she shares her preferences.

After they got married, Bill and Leah learned to do this on the topic of Christmas presents for his family. When they initially would discuss these presents, Leah had lots of ideas right away and Bill would say "fine with me," leaving Leah responsible for his family and without access to Bill's own ideas about what they might like. Then they developed a procedure where Bill would go first and Leah would hold off on her ideas until Bill had come up with some on his own. This created a better partnership on gift giving, with each feeling better about it. The same kind of thing can work for brides and grooms where the groom may need more time to articulate his hopes for the wedding.

7. *Don't make all your priorities the highest priority.* If a temptation for grooms is to say that nothing is a big deal (when some things are), the temptation for many brides is to see everything as a big deal, from the ceremony to the centerpieces. This does not make for good partnership and open negotiations. One way out of this trap is to ask yourself what is the core value underneath an urgent priority. For example, if you feel you must invite all of your wide network of relatives, friends, sorority sisters, and fellow townspeople to your wedding, but costs are going to run up higher than your groom is comfortable with, you can ask yourself whether your underlying value (to have a true community wedding) can be met by an alternative plan. Perhaps you can have a special party for the townspeople after the honeymoon, but not invite them to the wedding and reception.

8. *Talk about the main players and what to expect of them.*
    If you know that your mom is going to want to be
    heavily involved in the wedding planning, now is the
    time to bring it up. If you are concerned that your
    divorced parent may fight it out over the wedding,
    put it on the table. If one of your families is wealthy
    and likes extravagant weddings, mention that too.
    One groom we know did not mention to his bride
    the fact that his mother has a social phobia (very shy
    around strangers). The bride was quite distraught
    when his mother bailed out of the wedding shower at
    the last moment. She would have preferred an honest
    conversation many months prior, so that she could
    have prepared herself for his mother's no-show.

Understanding your ideals, expectations, and priorities
is the crucial first step in the wedding process. Write down
what you have agreed on thus far, knowing that some of it
may change over time. You are then prepared to talk with
relatives to get their perspectives, learn about what is feasible,
and prepare to make loads of decisions. You will know not only
what you hope for, but why and how strongly you want it. You
will know how you want to share leadership along the way, and
who is going to take major responsibility in different areas.

HOW DO YOU WANT TO PREPARE FOR YOUR MARRIAGE?

It's easy to get preoccupied with planning a wedding and
forget about what you can do to prepare in a more formal way
for your lifetime together. If you take no other advice in this
book, take this: Enroll in a premarital education program as
soon as possible. Even the strongest couples get a lot out of
premarital education. Sometimes you don't have a choice about

enrolling in a premarital program because your clergy person insists that you do. Other times it's up to you. In either case, it's up to you to decide how much you want to get out of the experience.

You may think you know each other well, and indeed you probably do. But in other ways you have barely scratched the surface, even if you have lived together for several years. There is more to learn about your personalities, strengths, weaknesses, family backgrounds, and values. A structured program can help you assess your strengths and challenges as a couple and offer you good communication tools for moving ahead in marriage.

Researchers have demonstrated the value of premarital education. Couples improve their communication and conflict skills and have happier relationships after they get married. The best premarital programs involve an inventory (questionnaire) combined with classes on communication and conflict resolution. The inventory will ask you each to answer questions about your values, beliefs, personalities, families, and other areas. The feedback you receive from a premarital educator is tailored to your specific relationship. For example, Mike and Elizabeth took the PREPARE inventory and participated in four premarital counseling sessions with a PREPARE-trained counselor. The PREPARE inventory helped them review the strengths and "growth areas" in their relationship, and the counseling sessions gave them instructions in effective communication. . You can visit our website (www. TheFirstDance.com) and take this inventory online to get a personalized report, without going to a counselor.

TALKING WITH YOUR PARENTS ABOUT THEIR EXPECTATIONS

Many couples discover their parents' hopes for the wedding in bits and pieces, and on the fly. You drop by their house to pick something up, or you call to arrange travel plans—and bang, you are talking about whether all twenty of your cousins will be on the guest list. Or worse, your parents have been doing some deep thinking about matters you have not thought through yet, such as who will perform the ceremony—and bang, they call to tell you that Rabbi Cohen is available. You stammer and maybe say, "Well, I guess that would be okay," only to regret it later and make your partner angry that you and your family made a unilateral decision. Here's a lesson for talking with parents about major wedding plans: *If you are not sitting down for a serious conversation, then it's just talk—nothing has been decided.*

We have a better idea: have a planned conversation to find out your parents' expectations and hopes for the wedding, what they want to contribute and what they want to happen. Explain that it could take an hour or more, and set a tone that this is an important and serious discussion. If you fail to set this tone, your parents may dismiss the idea of a meeting because they think there is plenty of time to make decisions. Explain that you do not want to make final decisions, but just to get their thoughts and feelings on the table as you move forward towards decisions. Half of your mission is already accomplished when they agree to the meeting and its agenda.

It is important, of course, to meet with each family separately, with both of you present and the blood relative leading the conversation. A meeting like this might feel strange between you and your parents; given the informality of most family conversations, it might be the first real "meeting" you have ever had with your parents when they were not disciplining you for something you did! Here is some language for requesting the meeting and for heading off a parent who wants to avoid having it:

> "Mom and Dad, Karen and I would like to sit down in the next week or so to get your thoughts about the wedding."
> (If you live out of town, then you would be asking for a time when you and your partner can visit or schedule a phone meeting.)
> "Ken, you are not getting married for 14 months! There is plenty of time."
> "I know, Mom, but we think this would be a good time to get ideas out on the table, before there is a lot of pressure. And some decisions are coming up soon, as you know."
> "Your father and I will support whatever you decide. It's going to be such a wonderful wedding. And your father and I have not even talked about it yet."
> "I know it's going to be a wonderful wedding. And I realize that you and Dad have not talked yet. We are not pushing for decisions, just to get your ideas before we get ahead of ourselves. Can we talk together this coming weekend for an hour or so?"
> "Well, I'll talk with your father about it."
> "I'll give you a call tomorrow to see if we can go ahead and meet this weekend."

This is a crucial conversation because you are acting like an adult who wants to have an adult conversation with your parents. If your parents are divorced, then you would ask for separate meetings. (More later on that.) Even if you are well into the wedding planning, you can ask for a meeting to discuss remaining issues.

When you get together, have an agenda of questions, preferably written down with copies for everyone. Turn off the television and make sure other family members are not around. Remind everyone that the goal is to get ideas and hopes out on the table, not necessarily to make decisions. If your parents try to derail the conversation again by saying something like, "It's your wedding, and we will support whatever you want," remind them that you want and need their input and help.

You might want to use the list of key planning issues in Table 3.1, using a standards question such as "What are your thoughts about (size of the wedding, location, etc.)" With parents, often a key expectation to get on the table is what they are prepared to contribute financially to the wedding. Even if you have talked about this before, go over it again. Do they have a specific dollar amount in mind, a general ballpark? Are they bankrolling all of the expenses, some of them, none of them? In our own case, Bill and Leah came up with a dollar amount of their contribution and said that Elizabeth and Mike should feel free to expand or contract specific costs within that overall budget. If one of your families has already decided what they are willing to pay for, you can share that with the other family.

Since costs are tied to the size of the guest list, now is an important time to get an idea of how many of their own family and friends your parents hope to invite to the wedding. Once again, the goal is not a decision on the size of the guest list, but a preliminary idea of everyone's expectations. This is where you might learn that in your in-law's town, weddings are for everyone you ever went to school with, or that your minister father feels obligated to invite his church board and fellow clergy in the community. You might learn that the bride's parents can contribute only a few thousand dollars but that the groom's parents are happy to cover the rest. Or that grandma has put away money for a big bash. On the other hand, you may learn that everyone believes that now that you are both 37 years old and making more money than your parents, you can pay for your own wedding and invite your parents to have ceremonial roles. The key is to uncover expectations before putting everything together into a set of decisions. Stifle your temptation to say, "How can you expect such a ridiculous thing?" Guideline: *No arguments when you are asking parents about their expectations and hopes; you are just gathering information.*

One way to avoid being drawn into an unnecessary conflict is to stress that the issue is something you have not yet reached a firm conclusion on. If your mother, after saying that she certainly hopes to invite all her family and friends to a big wedding in your home town, goes on to say with disapproval that she knows you want a small wedding in some remote mountain resort that her friends could never get to, you can reply "Yes, we've been talking abut that, but all options are on the table at the moment." Don't let yourself be forced into a decision you are not ready to make because you don't know all the circumstances; for example, if your parents want a big wedding in their favorite spot but are not willing to help pay for it, this might affect how much you want to bend their way. And a summer wedding in the mountains might attract more of her friends than a winter one.

If your parents are divorced, let each know that you are meeting with the other. This can be dicey if they don't talk to each other, putting you in the middle once more. One strategy some couples use successfully is to begin with the parent you think will be most involved and supportive during your wedding planning. Find out what this parent expects and is willing to contribute. Ask for permission to share this when you meet with the other parent. For example, Madeline's mother offered to pay for half of the wedding and reception expenses for a medium size wedding. When Madeline and her fiancé met with her father, they told him what her mother had offered. Relieved that he was not being expected to foot the whole bill, he readily agreed to handle his half. If the mother had declined to contribute, saying that she would help Madeline with mother of the bride responsibilities, but expected Madeline's father to handle all the costs, Madeline could have told her father that her mother was not going to contribute to the expenses. Madeline would be wise to not directly ask her father to cover everything, but rather use the meeting to learn what he is thinking. He may need some time to get over his resentment about his ex-wife's decision before deciding how much he would offer toward wedding expenses. In chapter five we will return to the challenges of dealing with divorced parents.

Maybe your divorced father (or mother) is likely to blurt out something like "I will not let your mother take advantage of me again by leaving me to hold the bag for your wedding." Every emotion in you wants you to break down in tears and scream, "You two are going to ruin my wedding like you ruined my childhood!" But if you are prepared for your father's remark, you can say something like this: "Dad, I am not expecting you to pay for my wedding. I just want your thoughts about whether you want to contribute to any of the expenses, and who you think we should be inviting." If he keeps criticizing your mother and saying how he is being screwed over once more, don't take the bait of defending your mother, as in "but she will help in other ways." (That will get you a quick negative retort that will make you feel like defending your mother or attacking your father.) Just repeat that you want to know his ideas for the wedding, and that he can think about it and talk later if he wants.

These painful encounters can be a way for you to become more grown up with your parents when they are not acting like grown ups. Things will go better if you have your fiancé sitting right there with you; you will feel stronger and your parents might be too embarrassed to behave at their worst. Their offers to help must come with no expectation that you will side with one against the other, as would be the case if your father said he would fund your wedding only if your mother kept her hands out of the planning. You have to be prepared to accept no financial help from either parent if you feel they are using you to battle each other. We will have lots more to say in the book about dealing with divorced parents. In the meantime, we turn next to how to handle disagreements between you and your fiancé about what kind of wedding to have.

CHAPTER FOUR

DEALING WITH YOUR DIFFERENCES AS A COUPLE

Sometimes weddings are like Greek tragedies: you end up bringing about exactly what you are trying to avoid. Tanya and Brett were determined to have a low-hassle wedding. They did not want to bother their relatives with the costs, and they wanted to avoid having to make hundreds of small decisions on their own. So they agreed to invite their immediate families (parents, siblings and siblings' spouses) to Tahoe for a simple wedding, no frills. It all seemed easy until Brett mentioned that he wanted to invite his godmother, Aunt Louise, who had practically been a second mother to him. Tanya put her foot down—no way was she going to expand the invitation list beyond their agreement. "Where would it end?" she kept asking. "But this is my one and only godmother," Brett retorted. "We have room for one more person, for crying out loud!" They argued for weeks, involving their families in the conflict. So much for a hassle-free wedding.

Here's another story: Jennifer was in charge of most of the wedding plans, but Sam had one "small" item he cared a lot about: the vehicle to transport them on the wedding day. He wanted something exotic like a Ferrari or a Porsche. "Absolutely not" was Jennifer's shocked response. He backed away and then brought it up again—and again. It seemed like a small concession to his dream of a wedding with some pizzazz. She could not believe he would be that insensitive.

In both scenarios, the couple did work out their differences, but only after too much conflict and stress. Tanya eventually thought to tell Brett her reasons for not inviting is favorite aunt: if they invited one aunt, they would have no good reason not to invite all nine of the aunts and uncles on both sides of the family. How could they justify favoring one over all the others? How could she not invite her mother's twin sister? Brett immediately understood once she explained what was beneath her strong objections. He had been missing the bigger picture of family fairness. It turned out that Brett's father also did not quite understand these things; when one of Brett's brothers-in-law had to cancel his trip to Tahoe, Brett's father argued for inviting Aunt Louise. Now that Brett and Tanya were together on the matter, Brett had no trouble explaining their policy, and the rationale, to his father.

As for Jennifer and Sam, they got past their vehicular conflict only after Jennifer broke down in tears during one of their arguments: "I won't be able to fit my dress in a Ferrari," she cried, "and an open convertible will ruin my hair!" She had never explained this to Sam, assuming he already understood a bride's logistical needs on her wedding day. Sam understood at last, apologized, and promised to order a stretch limo forthwith. He had been assuming that Jennifer wanted a limo just for the sake of tradition and was dismissing his desire for something funky. As with Tanya and Brett, the problem was not their difference of opinion but how they handled the difference. In both cases, the brides did not let the groom know what was beneath their ardent disagreement with what he as proposing, because they assumed he understood. On their part, the grooms assumed that the bride was just being picky or controlling, and did not ask what was beneath the objections. There is an old twist on the word "ASSUME": it makes an "ass" out of "u" and "me."

With all of the decisions you have to make as a couple, it's no wonder wedding planning is among the most stressful things you will ever do as a couple, up there with living with an infant and building a new house together. Weddings may be the worst because it seems that the entire world is watching. We have chosen four common areas of conflict to describe, not because everyone has them but because they can help to illuminate the underlying issues that most couples face when they disagree about their weddings.

THOSE BACHELOR PARTY BLUES

Look at chat rooms on the Internet and you will quickly find that plans for bachelor parties bring out intense emotions in brides. The gender gap looms large here. What to many grooms is just a lark, a traditional good time with the guys, is to many brides a hurtful and embarrassing betrayal. She is bothered by the idea that he will be getting drunk just before the wedding, but mostly by the strip club expedition that is part of many bachelor parties. He in turn is bothered that she is making such a big deal out of the guy-only part of the wedding. He and his friends have been out drinking many times before, and the strippers are not a threat to his future bride or to their marriage.

What's underneath this conflict? How can they understand where each is coming from, so that they can keep this issue from dividing them? For many grooms, the bachelor party is something they feel they don't have much control over; they just show up for what their friends have planned. It's hard to tell your friends what they can and cannot do for your bachelor party without seeming, well, uptight and ungrateful. Brides might try to understand this by thinking about how little control they have over a traditional bridal shower; you show up and go with the flow.

But as a bride you may retort that your wedding shower does not involve male strippers! (Actually, some bachelorette parties involve male strippers, but let's assume this is not for you.) It's important for you to do two things: explain your feelings to your fiancé, and try to understand his. The goal should be to "de-fang" the bachelor party, to take the poison out of your relationship, rather than to have one of you win and the other lose. So tell your guy that you feel threatened that he will be ogling other women right before your wedding, that you feel disrespected as his future wife, and that you worry about him being drunk and hung over during a time when you need his full energy and attention. If you trust him but not his friends, say that. But then listen to his side rather than indignantly digging in your heels.

For grooms, we urge you to listen to your fiancée's feelings rather than dismissing them as an over-reaction. (Clue for guys: swear off now and forever telling your wife that she is overreacting; this is patronizing and backfires every time.) What is a small matter for you may have a strong impact on her. Instead, tell her you understand that she feels threatened and distrustful, and that you feel badly that she is upset. (Only say these things, of course, if you mean them.) Then tell her why the bachelor party is important to you, for example, that it's a ritual you want to do with your friends and something they want to do for you. You can say that you would feel ungrateful if you told them to not have a party for you. What's more, even if you told them to skip the strip club part, you are not sure they would comply. What would you do if, after a good meal and some games, they insisted on taking you to the local strip club? Could you make a fuss and go home? Not likely. Your own preference, given your fiancée's feelings, would be to skip the stripper part of the evening, but you may not have control over that. What you do have control over is how much alcohol you consume personally and how you behave at the strip joint if that is part of your friends' plan. You also have some control over the timing of the bachelor party, which you could ask to occur a few weeks before the wedding rather than a few days, so that it is over with before the intensity of the wedding preparations kicks in.

This way of handling a bachelor party is not hypothetical. It's how Elizabeth and Mike handled what started out as a strong conflict over the plans for his bachelor party. They came to a compromise after they both felt understood. Elizabeth decided to not make a big deal of it after Mike acknowledged her feelings and assured her that he was going along with a tradition that he could try to tone down but not control. He told her he thought the stripper thing was silly. It turns out that he and his friends had a good meal, drank a bit, played "paintball" for many hours, and put in a brief appearance as the local strip club before calling it an evening. And it was well before the wedding and a non-issue for Mike and Elizabeth.

YOUR RELIGION, MY RELIGION

If bachelor party conflicts can be painful, at least they mostly involve just the couple in their private conversations. Religious differences are a different matter altogether because they involve the big three: family, faith, and community. In the United States, weddings and religion tend to go hand in hand. The vast majority of first marriages in the United States are held in religious settings, and in a country where people practice many different religions, it's common that couples come from different faith traditions.

It's also common for one partner to be religious and the other not. Carla and Tom did not talk much about religion until they got engaged. She was an active Methodist, while he considered himself a religious skeptic. Their first argument was over the premarital counseling sessions required for couples who wanted to get married at her church. Tom gave in, but told her he thought the whole thing was a joke. Carla was afraid that Tom would be rude to the pastor and embarrass her—or even provoke the pastor into refusing to do the wedding. Before talking with Tom, Carla asked other brides for advice on a web chat room.

Carla received some good advice. Several people pointed out that if he was not mature enough to be respectful in a counseling session, there were bigger problems to deal with! Several brides said that their fiancés were like Tom but behaved appropriately with the priest or minister. Others pointed to the larger challenge lying ahead: one spouse wanting to be religiously active, and to raise the children that way, with the other being actively negative about religion. (One bride in the chat room wrote that her partner haughtily maintains that the only reason churches want good attendance is for the collection envelope; how is that going to play when his wife leaves for church on a Sunday morning with the kids?) What Carla and Tom need is a deeper conversation about their core values and their ability to respect (not just tolerate and certainly not disdain) their differences. We strongly recommend they take a premarital inventory such as PREPARE (available through www.TheFirstDance.com) or RELATE (www.relate-institute. org) and see a premarital counselor. Their differences are bigger than the wedding.

Another couple with a complicated situation worked it out well. Laura had been raised in a liberal Protestant church, considered herself moderately religious, but was not a regular churchgoer. Dan had been raised in a devout Catholic family but was now questioning some aspects of his religious tradition; however, it was important to him and to his family that the Catholic Church bless his marriage. They were to be married in Laura's hometown where she wanted a minister friend of the family, whom she had known all her life, to perform the wedding. Dan did not have a favorite priest but he was firm on a Catholic wedding. To make things trickier, Laura did not want to sign the required promise to raise their future children in the Catholic faith. Other people told her that the pledge was just a formality, not something enforceable. Dan himself was willing to sign because it was part of being married in the church, even though he was not sure he would remain a Catholic and raise his children in this faith. But for Laura it was a big deal; she could not see herself making a promise she did not intend to keep.

Fortunately, this couple was able to talk openly with each other about their feelings and wishes; each respected the other's stance as they tried to figure a way out of their dilemma. They set about investigating their options until they came up with one that worked. They did their premarital counseling with a Catholic deacon whom they both liked very much, someone who understand their situation. He agreed to come to their wedding at Laura's church and be part of the ceremony in a way that would be comfortable for the minister whom Laura wanted to perform the service. Laura did not have to make a promise to raise the children Catholic, but she did not object to Dan making the promise. The result was a wedding that was meaningful to both the bride and groom (and both of their families) because it reflected their faith traditions and the current state of their religious lives. They also ended up with two clergymen whom they liked and respected—and probably a greater openness to their religious future together than if they had polarized around their differences or if either had "won" the struggle.

We see here what can happen when couples are open with their differences and the reasons behind them, and listen respectfully. It opens up ways to investigate options that at first do not seem possible. When you know what each of you feels and wants at a deep level, you can be creative about finding ways to meet both of your needs. It won't turn out exactly the way either of you though it would, but neither does marriage! We know one couple who had two weddings—a Christian service and a Hindu service—combined with two receptions. It was exhausting but served the needs of both spouses and their families.

STRUGGLES OVER FOLLOW THROUGH

Brides frequently complain that their groom does not follow through on the things he has agreed to do. For example, he agrees to get a guest list from his parents but procrastinates bringing it up to them. Or he brings it up once but does not follow through when they delay. Meanwhile, the bride and her parents are growing nervous about how big the wedding is going to be, how much it will cost, and how many people they can invite from their side. The bride feels helpless because the groom is the one who should talk with his own parents; she cannot make this happen on her own. So she resorts to nagging, and he responds evasively (saying he is working on it) or angrily (tell her to stop bugging him). No fun for anyone.

Other times it's an important but less urgent matter such as ordering the limo, another task that grooms traditionally take on. In Wendy and Jon's wedding planning, she was the operational manager and he had just a few tasks, including the limo. Jon was a chronic procrastinator, something Wendy knew. She kept planting hints that the good limos would be reserved months ahead of the June wedding, but he kept postponing making the calls. He finally did check out prices, they talked about what they wanted, but then delayed sealing the deal, claiming there was still a lot of time. When he finally tried to reserve a limo, all that was left was a dinky vehicle that would hardly hold her and her gown. Wendy was furious up to and including her wedding day.

We realize that these examples are about insistent brides and procrastinating grooms, and not vice versa. While we recognize that it can go the other way, most of the conflicts we see reflect the tendency of brides to be more preoccupied with the details of wedding planning while grooms feel less urgency. It's the culture we live in and are raised in. Unfortunately, it sets up a stressful scenarios and patterns of nagging and resistance that carry over into marriage. Next we offer you strategies for avoiding this upsetting gridlock during your wedding planning.

HOW TO TALK ABOUT YOUR DIFFERENCES

Differences and disagreements are as inevitable in wedding planning as they are in marriage itself. So this is a good time to learn how to deal with them. There is lots of research showing that it's how you deal with conflict, more than what you have conflict about, that is the key to a successful marriage. Here are some strategies you might find helpful:

1. *Lay out the complete picture that each decision connects to.*
   You can avoid many of the problems we discussed in this chapter if you fully discuss how each decision in a wedding affects all the other decisions. For example, the guest list is crucial to know before many of the other decisions are made because it affects decisions

about facilities and costs, among other things. This can motivate a slow moving partner to take action. If one of you wants a tropical beach vacation and the other a home town wedding, you can discuss these options in the light of other issues such as the fact that both of you want your frail grandparents to come to your wedding. Seeing the larger picture can help you resolve your differences.

2. *Ask yourselves who cares more about the issue.* Sometimes you can decide to gracefully give up your personal preference because the matter is a bigger deal for your partner. You always imagined a small, intimate wedding but your partner cherishes the family tradition of big bashes. As long as you can work out the finances, why not sign up for a big wedding and enjoy yourself, rather than fighting over each new name added to the list?

3. *Ask yourself who is more stressed over the issue and who is good at the task.* If the groom is anxious about deciding on the tuxedos, why should he have to do this alone? The bride can be part of this decision and help the groom order the tuxes; they both will feel better about it. Sometimes procrastination comes from a sense of insecurity about making a mistake. In one case, the groom had a better sense of color than the bride, and he cared more about the aesthetics of the wedding. They agreed that he would work closely with the bride on all the aesthetics of the wedding and the reception, to her great relief. In this case, why not go with your abilities instead of with tradition?

4. *Teach and learn from one another rather than assuming the other "gets it."*
   Sometimes one of you will not see a problem that is quite clear to the other. This occurred in the earlier

story when the groom insisted on inviting his favorite aunt to the small wedding. Rather than waiting for a blow-up, the bride could have explained her entire rationale to her partner early in their conversations. You can both educate each other about your families and their traditions. The groom from a Hindu family should explain to his Christian bride what is involved in a traditional Hindu wedding, rather than having surprises keep coming up piecemeal.

5.   *When someone is not following through, consider agreeing to take the matter out of that person's hands.* In one couple, the groom knew more about photography but since the bride and her mother were paying for it, they felt they should be the ones to find a good photographer. The groom was growing impatient about the delay, about where they were looking for recommendations, and about how they were weighing the costs. In this case, why not agree that the one who is most stressed about the situation takes it over, especially if that person has the ability to follow through? In the same way, if the groom is not lining up the limo, and the bride is losing sleep over it, she can nicely say that it would be a big relief to her if he let her just go ahead and make the reservation. The key is to do this without rancor and to agree together on a shift of responsibility, rather than saying "Since you won't do it, I will!" And then the person who has been relieved of one responsibility should offer to help with other responsibilities.

6.   *When you are doing your best to deal with your differences and yet remain polarized, consider whether deeper issues are underlying your conflict.* For example, sometimes the issue is not about the size of the wedding but about a feeling of envy or competition because one of you has a bigger family or circle of friends. Try

asking gently if your partner is feeling envious or insecure about this difference. Sometimes the issue is not between the two of you, but between one of you and your family, as when a groom kept insisting on an extremely informal reception without speeches but was not saying that he was afraid of being embarrassed by his father getting near a microphone. In the chapter on working with family conflicts, we will describe hidden issues that make even simple decisions fraught with unnecessary conflict.

7. *The standard tools of effective communication are particularly important when there is tension between you.* Examples are speaking for yourself using "I-statements" rather than attacking the other person, listening to understand before proposing solutions, and choosing the best time and place to talk about difficult matters. Your everyday communication patterns might be fine for everyday matters, but when you are negotiating a wedding, it's good to be at your best. There are many excellent marriage education programs that offer classes on these communication skills. Find them at www.smartmarriages.com and www.healthymarriageinfo.org.

Almost no couple gets through planning a wedding without a few good meltdowns. But if you stick together, make decisions as a team, and support each other with your families and friends, nothing can stop you from having a wedding you will feel proud of forever. We literally mean that *nothing* and *nobody* can stop you from feeling good about your wedding if you forge a solid bond of loving teamwork. Torrential rain may fall off season, relatives may embarrass you or try to fight old battles through you, the florist may go belly-up the week before your wedding, and the bridesmaid may need an emergency appendectomy the day before your wedding—but if you stick together through it all, these will just be good stories to tell your children someday. And if you keep your balance and good cheer during the amazing journey ahead, your loved ones too will say it was the wedding of their dreams.

CHAPTER FIVE

HANDLING DIFFERENCES WITH YOUR FAMILIES

"What? Two thousand dollars for a dress you will wear just once? That's obscene!"

"We don't care how many cousins your fiancé's family feel they have to invite, they will just have to stay within the number of guests we gave them."

"I can't believe her parents are so chintzy. Tell them we will pay for the flowers so that the wedding doesn't look second rate."

"When your grandmother finds out you are not marrying in the church, it will kill her."

"If your mother and her boyfriend come to your wedding, I will not show up. It's your choice."

Ask newlywed couples what were the trickiest parts of their wedding planning and the majority will tell you it was not dealing with caterers, photographers or wedding planners—it was the relatives. This should not surprise anyone. A wedding is the grandest family event, the family's main act on the big stage. It generally costs a sizable amount of money, it involves nearly everyone important to the family, it puts the family's tastes and values on public display, it often involves religion, it launches a major change in family relationships, it brings together two family clans who did not know each other, and it involves hundreds of decisions made by different combinations of people who care deeply that everything comes off beautifully—and affordably.

On top of these standard family dynamics surrounding weddings, add the idiosyncrasies and flaws of family members on both sides. The bride's mother who never got to plan her own wedding and now is determined to have her way with yours. The bride's stubborn, practical father who complains vocally every time he hears a price. The bride's competitive sister who is outraged that she is not the maid of honor. The groom's mother who is the maven of good taste and frequent commentator on decisions outside of her influence. The stepmother on either side who is determined to stick it to her husband's "ex." This is the stuff of theatre, and the script has many authors. You can't write the whole script, just your own part, but how you handle your role may determine whether the inevitable struggles and mishaps turn out as comedy or tragedy. We want to help you play your part in family disagreements with integrity; in so doing, you just might bring out the best instead of the worst in your fellow family members.

FIGURING OUT WHAT'S GOING ON

Some family disagreements are inevitable in planning a wedding; no two people are going to spontaneously agree on the hundreds of decisions involved. We have listed a number of common conflict areas in Table 5.1, ranging from early decisions such as the date of the wedding to later decisions such as the invitations. Sometimes the sources of these disagreements are straightforward—for example, differences in styles, tastes, or even schedules—and other times they run deeper, for example, family loyalty about who should be invited to the wedding. We like to make a distinction between routine conflicts that can be resolved amicably after a couple of conversations, and deeper conflicts that leave everyone feeling hurt and misunderstood. Routine conflicts lend themselves to compromise. You want an artsy cake and your mother wants a traditional one, and you settle on something in between. You want a small wedding and your parents (who are paying) want to invite everyone they ever met; you compromise somewhere in between. Routine conflicts also lend themselves to one side coming around to other's position after reflecting on it. You wanted to get married on January 2 and your parents convinced you that holiday and school schedules make it too difficult for family members who will be traveling to the wedding; you set the date later in the month. Although there may be a few tense moments during a routine conflict, basically you feel good that you worked it out with everyone feeling heard and understood.

Table 5.1

DIFFICULT CONFLICT WITH PARENTS

Here are some major areas of conflict that occur between engaged couples and their parents. Following them is a list of issues or concerns that may underlie conflicts that don't seem to get resolved—the disagreements that come up over and over and lead to hurt feelings.

Areas of Conflict
1. Location of the wedding
2. Date and time
3. Style of invitations
4. Style of wedding ceremony
5. Money/budget
6. Number of guests
7. Invitation list
8. Bride's Dress
9. Food and drink at reception

10. Photographer
11. Music
12. Who officiates
13. Cake
14. Wedding party (number, specific people)

Then there are the deeper conflicts, often over the same issues, that drive you up the wall. For these conflicts, you have to look at possible underlying sources in order to understand what is going on and how to deal with it. You know that you are dealing with a deeper conflict when the following things are going on:

- There are raised voices every time you discuss the matter.
- Someone shuts down and won't talk about the matter anymore.
- You are not feeling heard, or your parents are not feeling heard.
- You are stalemated; there is no progress after two or three conversations.
- You or your parents are feeling personally attacked.
- Language is getting inflammatory ("I don't care for..." becomes "I can't stand...")
- Third parties are getting pulled into the conflict (as in "Your sisters agree with me that the cake you want is gross.")

When conflicts have some of these ingredients, the solution may require figuring out the underlying fears, concerns, or values that are driving the disagreement, and dealing with those. In other words, the way out of the impasse starts with an effort to understand what is driving it. Say your mother can't abide the wedding invitations you like. She gripes about the color, the font, the size of the envelopes, and the wording. You find yourself defending your taste under an onslaught of criticism that ends with your mother saying something passive aggressive such as, "But it's your wedding; you're old enough to know what you want." Of course you could just go ahead with the invitations, especially if you are paying for them yourselves, but you feel badly about just overriding your mother's objections. (And you worry that she will harbor a grudge and make life difficult on future decisions.) But the discussions go nowhere when you say, "The font is large enough to read; I showed it to some of my friends," and your mother shoots back, "Your friends have younger eyes than my friends, and whoever saw yellow wedding invitations?" "They are goldenrod," you volley back. If the coming year is going to be this way, you think, eloping looks mighty attractive.

Rather than give in or just override your mother's views, you can try to understand concerns that she may or may not be voicing. We are assuming for the moment that your mother is not congenitally negative and controlling; if she is, then you need a different strategy we will discuss later in the book. The following strategies usually work with relatives who are being difficult but who are not impossible people.

Your first task, again, is to figure out what is not being put clearly on the table. When people seem irrationally negative or stubborn, there is usually an underlying fear or concern. For weddings, here are some underlying concerns of parents that that can fuel conflicts. The unexpressed concerns may be yours as well; don't overlook the possibility that you are the one being irrationally negative or stubborn. Look at Table 5.2 for common messages, usually not clearly expressed, that underlie many difficult conflicts during the planning of a wedding. If a strong disagreement you are having with a parent (or someone else) does not make sense to you, ask yourself whether someone may have one of the feelings we outline in the table.

Table 5.2

SOME UNDERLYING SOURCES OF WEDDING CONFLICTS

Ask yourself (or your parents, if your relationship is good enough) if one or more of the following issues might be underlying a difficult conflict.

1. I feel like I don't count to you; my needs, wishes, and values don't seem to matter.
2. I will be embarrassed in front of my people.
3. My side of the family is being treated unfairly.
4. I am being taken advantage of by my ex-spouse.
5. My religious values are being compromised.
6. I can't afford what you are asking for.
7. If I do this for you, I will feel disloyal to someone else.
8. I thought this was mostly my decision and now you have made it.
9. I am not getting enough credit for the time and money I am putting into this wedding.
10. I am ambivalent (or negative) about this wedding: either about the person you are marrying or about the fact that you are getting married at this moment in your life.

In the case of wedding invitations, we know a family in which the bride's mother feared that the non-traditional invitations signaled that the entire wedding would be something that she and her family and friends would feel uncomfortable attending. She blurted this out when her daughter, during melt down argument, burst into tears and asked, "Why are you being so mean about me wanting these lovely invitations?" Her mother then let out her real fear: "I don't want to be the mother of the bride of a hippie wedding! I want it to have some dignity!" Her daughter then reassured her that the wedding would be mostly traditional—flower girls, bridesmaids, an organ, the works—but that she and her fiancé wanted to have more contemporary invitations. Her mother took in this reassurance, and came to accept the invitations with some degree of grace.

The bride and groom could perhaps have cut short this painful chapter on the invitations if, after the initial flurry of conflict, they had tried to sort out what mother was really worried about. One way to do this is by asking a direct question. During a calm moment, away of any controversial topics, pop the question: "Mom, I know you are not happy with the invitations we are thinking of choosing. Could you tell me what your biggest concern is?" To ask this question constructively, you have to be ready for an answer that may trouble you, as in "I don't want this to be a hippie wedding," or "My friends will think it's off the wall." If you have guessed that this might be her answer, then you can be prepared to reassure her that there are lots of decisions ahead, that many of them will come out in ways that she and her friends will find familiar and comforting, and that in fact you and she share many of the same wishes for the wedding. (If you and your parent have strikingly different visions of the wedding, this should have been made clear at the outset of the wedding planning [see chapter three], in which case you would not even be in this dialogue about the invitations.)

Sometime parents cannot or will not tell you what is most troubling them. They will stay fixated on the details, like the color of the invitations or the cake, or they will just clam up. In that case, you can try to elicit the concern they are afraid to voice, as in "I wonder if you are worried that we are going to end up with a hippie wedding." Or "Are you afraid that everything about this wedding is going to seem foreign to you and your friends?" There is a good chance that she will come clean if you ask the question in a sensitive, loving way. Then you can try to reassure her instead of arguing defensively about the invitations.

Use Table 5.2 as a guide to trying to figure out what might be the underlying concerns family members might bring to conflicts over wedding plans. Here's a rule of thumb: if the disagreement cannot be resolved in a couple of conversations, and if it gets more polarized with further discussion, then there is an issue underlying that is not being expressed. If you can't put the concern on the table, it bites everyone under the table. Getting it out in the open does not mean that simple reassurance will always resolve the disagreement, as it did in the wedding invitation example; we'll talk later about other strategies. But at least you know what you are dealing with—and it's not the icing on the cake.

NEGOTIATING DIFFERENCES WITH YOUR PARENTS

After focusing on what the real issues are, the second key to resolving differences with families is to be clear for yourselves about which decisions are subject to revision—and therefore negotiable—and which decisions are final and not negotiable. Presumably most should be in the first category, based on the premise that there is rarely only one correct way to do something. Maybe you would like to have all the wedding photos done before the service, but your mother argues that it will be too taxing on grandma to arrive an hour before the service. So you do the photos with grandma after the service. Your father says that his Uncle Charlie really, really wants to do his skit at the groom's dinner—the one he does at all the weddings. You think it's corny and will take away from the classiness of the occasion, but you go along, bearing in mind that no one remembers these events anyway. The salmon was by far the best dish the caterer serves, but your parents draw the line at $30 per plate and you settle for the chicken Kiev, bearing in mind that no one remembers the food at receptions. You really would prefer your best friend as your maid of honor, but your mother begs you not to dishonor your sister by excluding her from this role in the wedding. Your sister says she does not care, but it's obvious your mother does. So you go along, bearing in mind that a good friend will understand. You go along without rancor or a sense of being victimized, because you realize that your wedding has many stakeholders and it's OK to bend on the things that are not at the core of your values.

Other times, just giving in does not work for you because you care more about this part of the wedding. You then use your negotiation skills. As you learn what good wedding photographers cost, your parents get skittish about paying for the quality of photos that you prefer. Rather than make this a standoff, you can look at the underlying concerns on both sides and negotiate accordingly. Your parents' concerns are monetary, yours are aesthetic. There are a couple of ways to negotiate this. One is to reassure your parents that you will stay within the wedding budget agreed to earlier, and will cut costs on other aspects of the wedding to offset the higher than expected photography expenses. Another is to say that you would like to pay for the photography yourselves, since you realize that this expense is considerably more than your parents had counted on. Of course, you have to make this offer with an open heart and not with resentment. Here is some language for this conversation:

"Mom and Dad, we've been thinking about the photography costs and agree with you that they are higher than any of us thought they would be, and we want to stay within budget. What we'd like to do is to handle the wedding photography costs ourselves, and that way we can all stop worrying about how we will have to cut costs in other parts of the wedding. We are handling the honeymoon, and we'd like to handle the photography. Would that be all right with you?"

If you can't offer to cover an expense with this kind of spirit, then don't try. Your parents will feel you are being passive aggressive, offering to pay it yourself while expecting them to decline your offer. But if you can negotiate this as adults with adults, it is likely to lead to a good outcome—either your parents accept your decision or you all agree to watch the other expenses and try to not break the bank.

Then there are the big decisions that are not negotiable. This will differ for each couple, so our examples may not apply to you. It may be very important to you that the wedding ceremony reflect the religious traditions of both spouses. Sometimes this can be accommodated in one ceremony, even though relatives on either side might be uncomfortable. Other times this will require something more radical—we know a couple who had two ceremonies: a Christian one and a Hindu one. In either case, your parents and relatives will just have to accept your decision and make the best of it. Your job is not to ask if they are OK with your decision but to keep them informed about what to expect at an unfamiliar religious service. Later we will deal with the situation where someone threatens a boycott.

Another rule of thumb: do not ask for feedback on decisions that are not negotiable. That sends a mixed message to your family. Don't ask, "How would you feel about having a rabbi do the service with our minister" if you have already decided the matter, and it's agreeable to the two clergy persons. Just say, "We want to let you know that we have lined up David's rabbi and our minister to do the service." If your parents complain about the arrangement later on when you are discussing the details of the service, you can gently remind them that it's a done deal. Most people find a way to accept that which is inevitable when, "resistance is futile." On your end, you may have to accept the fact that your parents do not fully support your decision, and then not seek their emotional approval. It's part of being emotionally ready for marriage.

NEGOTIATING DIFFERENCES ACROSS FAMILIES

Conflict between the bride's and groom's families are some of the trickiest parts of wedding planning. Table 5.3 lists common areas of conflict and possible sources of conflicts that keep coming up and cause hurt feelings.

For Maria and Jason's wedding, the big problem was the guest list. The head count had been set month before, but now Jason's mother asked to invite twenty additional people from her work setting. At fifty dollars per person for the banquet, this request shocked the bride's parents, who were already concerned about the size of the wedding based on the mother's large and boisterous Latino family. In fact, this was one of the reasons the groom's divorced mother wanted her friends along; she thought she would feel overwhelmed by this large family from a different culture (she was an only child from a soft spoken Norwegian family and had few relatives) and wanted support from her coworkers since she did not have a husband to support her at the event. After some struggle and hurt feelings on both sides, the issue was resolved in a way that serves as a good example of wedding negotiations:

- The groom's mother was clear about what need she was trying to meet by inviting twenty new guests. She was not arguing that these were her dearest friends in the world or that she owed them because they had all invited her to their kids' weddings. Her need for support was out on the table.

- The bride's parents' issue was also out on the table: the unanticipated expense of feeding twenty extra people. Although they wondered privately why this woman felt the need for so many support people, they wisely kept these concerns to themselves and certainly did not share them with the groom, who would have felt defensive for his mother.

- The bride and groom suggested a middle ground: to invite the group of ten coworkers but not their spouses or partners. This would give the mother the same access to support people (her coworkers were her friends, not their significant others) and would be less expensive for the bride's parents. This solution involved some bending of protocol for invitations to a wedding, which calls for inviting a spouse or partner of the invitee's choice. The deal involved the groom's mother willingness to take responsibility for explaining the situation to her co-workers, which she was willing to do.

- The whole situation would have been better if the groom's mother initially had been more sensitive to the expense she was asking the other family to incur, instead of just announcing her wishes. She could have offered to pay for the extra guests, and allowed the bride's parents to graciously decline, or better yet, she could have told her son that she was feeling the need for more support people, and then problem solved this with him instead of announcing her solution. For example, they might have come up with the idea of inviting two or three people that she is closest to, instead of everyone on her work team. But having missed those opportunities for collaborative problem solving, at least she was willing to compromise on the final number and take the heat for not inviting spouses and partners.

This scenario points to guidelines for managing conflicts between families in wedding planning, which (next to divorce situations) are the most delicate challenges most couples face. The key is for everyone to keep both families' needs and perspectives in mind from the start. It doesn't matter who is paying for the wedding—the couple, the bride's parents or the groom's parents. Both families are stakeholders. When one of them feels they don't count or are being treated unfairly, it's trouble for everyone—and not a good way to start a marriage.

Table 5.3

AREAS OF CONFLICT BETWEEN YOUR FAMILIES

Common Areas of Conflict

1. Religious differences
2. Guest list
3. Money—who pays for what

4. Money—differences in how families spend
5. Regional differences in wedding expectations
6. Cultural differences in wedding expectations

Possible Underlying Sources of Conflict

1. Feeling left out
2. Feeling unfairly burdened
3. Not getting enough credit for contributions to the wedding
4. Fear of losing one's child to the other family
5. Sense that one's culture is not being respected
6. Sense that one's religion is not being respected
7. Feeling "shown up" by the other family's greater wealth
8. Doubts about the suitability of the new spouse

An unfortunately common scenario is that the bride and her family dictate the terms of the wedding arrangements to the groom's family. We think it's a mistake to give decrees such as how many guests the other family can invite, without a dialogue first to find out how many they want to invite. Even 50-50 arrangements of guests can feel unfair if one family has a huge clan and the other just a few living relatives. Sometimes one early decision, such as where to hold the reception, constrains future decisions and leads to one family feeling left out. For example, your decision to have the reception in a beautiful but small place may mean that the groom's parents cannot invite beloved relatives or life long friends whose family weddings they themselves have attended. This implication had not occurred to you or the bride's parents when choosing the facility, perhaps because you knew the bride's network would be easily accommodated. That's why we recommend getting the big picture of everyone's expectations before making any decisions that seriously constrain future options. That's not to say that everyone's expectations have to be fulfilled, but it is a lot more sensitive to let the parents of the groom know early on that it will be a small wedding so that they can let their network know, rather than dealing with the fallout months later when you say, "Oh by the way, you can only invite forty people, which is all we can handle and which will work fine for the other family."

WHEN YOUR PARENTS ARE DIVORCED

Far and away the most difficult negotiations occur with parents who are divorced. It seems not to matter if the divorce occurred a year ago or twenty years ago, although current spouses and boyfriends/girlfriends always make things more complicated no matter when the divorce happened. Let's begin with a positive story, one that can help you appreciate your divorced parents and stepparents when they do come through for you. Marsha had raised Becky since infancy, along with Becky's father. Becky's mother Sue had been in and of her daughter's life but now wanted back in for the wedding. Although Becky was far closer to her stepmother, she accepted her mother's wishes and made her the central person for the wedding planning and the wedding ceremony (despite the fact that Sue was paying for little of the event). Marsha felt sick about being cast aside in favor of a woman she felt had been a poor mother over the years; Marsha felt that she herself had been Becky's real mother.

It helped enormously that Marsha was a woman of uncommon maturity and insight, and that her husband, Becky's father, was very supportive. She realized that Becky was trying to draw her mother back into her life, afraid that if she did not make her mother the central wedding figure, she would be gone again from Becky's life. (Marsha was her secure female parent.) Unfortunately, Becky was not able to say this to Marsha; she was probably not consciously aware of her complex feelings. Marsha decided to absorb the hurt and not lay a guilt trip on Becky. She did not turn the wedding into a loyalty bid for Becky by competing with her mother. She stayed on the sidelines, managing her grief and resentment with the support of her husband and friends. She could have ruined the wedding for Marsha by going to battle with Sue, but she acted like a good mother, with the hope that someday, perhaps when Becky has children, the two of them can talk openly about it.

Sadly, many divorced parents and stepparents are not able or willing to keep their child's needs first in the crucible of a wedding. Negotiations can make the Middle East seem like child's play. We have some ideas to help you make the best of the situation and to keep yourself and your couple relationship intact. To start, let's go back to our first principle: understand what the deeper issues are behind stubborn or irrational demands. Here are a few common issues that underlie conflicts in divorced families as they deal with a wedding:

- Because I raised you, my needs and desires come first.
- Because I did not get a chance to raise you, I will not be sidelined now.
- I gave that woman so much money over the years, I'm not spending a dime more for this fancy wedding she wants to put on.
- I spent so much money raising you, that cheapskate can come through now.

- That woman your father left me for has ruined my life, and I won't have her ruin this wedding.
- That man your mother left me for has ruined by life, etc.
- Your father/mother insisting on bringing along their new "friend" is a direct slap at me on this happy day.
- I'm your mother. I will not be upstaged by your stepmother.

Notice that the couple getting married are not central to these concerns; the drama unfolds mainly between the ex-spouses who are often unaware that they are putting their own needs way ahead of their children's. The wedding is either the latest act in their longstanding struggle or it activates earlier grief and resentment between parents who may have been doing fairly well in recent years. In either case, you will do better with your parents if you can empathize with the pain and hurt that underlies their difficult behavior—and then deal with them with both compassion and firmness. In some ways, you have to be the parent here when your parents are acting like hurt children. Sometimes, of course, it's just one parent acting badly, with the other parents able to manage the complex feelings and be there for you. That parent is a treasure, something you should let him or her know.

Here's our advice, not based on personal experience like so much else in this book, but based on what we've learned from watching and talking with others, and from Bill's experience as a therapist.

1. Remind yourself that you cannot control your parents. You can only take responsibility for your own actions. Ultimately, they will each play this out as they personally decide.

2. Keep in mind that the rest of the world sees your parents as responsible for themselves. In the worse case scenario (it's good to think about this), if they behave horribly in public, no one will blame you; they will feel sorry for you.

3. If you are focusing on the demanding behavior of one of your stepparents, your anger is probably misplaced—it should be focused on your parent who is permitting their partner to act badly and who is not standing up for you. Sometimes the stepparent is actually the stand in for the parent who is too chicken to make trouble directly. Talk first (and firmly) with your parent, not your stepparent.

4. Your main job is to clearly define for yourself and others what you want and need, and what you will accept and not accept in your parents' behavior. For example, if your father continually says, "Your mother always gets her way anyway," don't defend your mother but rather challenge your father: "Dad, that kind of line bothers me and is not helpful in planning this wedding. Would you please stop?" When your mother says, "I wonder what your father's latest bimbo will wear to the wedding," you can cut her off at the pass with "Mom, I'm not going to be catty with you. Say that kind of thing to your friends."

5. Negotiate openly with both sides. Agree to keep no secrets. If there are disagreements about how many people will be invited from each side of the family, be open about that fact and suggest everyone negotiate as adults. If your mother wants clarity about who will be in what family photos, let everyone know

that this issue has come up, and work on a solution in advance of the wedding day. There are rarely any surprise concerns in divorced families; the roles and scripts are well known.

6. When discussing extended family, don't allow the conversation to get sidetracked into comments about who turned against whom during the divorce. Remind your parents that the other parent may not be their family anymore, but they are still your family.

7. You probably have more clout than you realize, because deep down your parents probably do cherish you and want you to have a good wedding. Your best appeal is not for understanding of an "ex" but for understanding that you do not want to be in the middle and that you need support during an exciting but difficult time in your life. "Do it for me" can be your mantra. Most of the time, both divorced and non-divorced parents alike will rally and support their kids, swallowing what they have to swallow. But what if they don't? That's what we turn to next.

WHEN FAMILY MEMBERS MAKE THREATS OR ULTIMATUMS

Here we are talking about two kinds of situations: minor threats and major ones. The first is when someone is being passive-aggressive about a decision that cannot be reversed. You decided months ago on the menu, and now your grandmother declares, "This food is going to be so fancy I won't eat a bit of it." Ignore grandma, or say "More for the rest of us," if you can get away with saying it playfully. Sometimes a relative has a track record making histrionic statements like, "I'm sure I will faint in the aisle of a church that does not worship the one true God." Bring smelling salts. Often these relatives don't make the comment to you directly, but someone else in the family has the poor judgment to pass it on to you. Sometimes the one who passes on the comment has the same objection, but is hiding behind someone else. Don't engage. Laugh it off.

The second kind is more serious and has to be engaged: a threat by parents to boycott the wedding if they do not get their way. In intact families, the most common scenario is religious, when you marry someone outside the faith or when you marry outside of the family's religious setting. Again, the first step is to seek to understand. Some traditionally religious parents believe that they are putting their own souls at risk by participating in another religious service. This is not the teaching of any major religion, and you can ask your parents to check with their religious leader to confirm that. In other words, no religion we are aware of decrees punishment for a parent who sits through a child's wedding in a different faith tradition.

The issue is more likely that the parents do not accept the fact that their child is marrying outside of the faith and are registering their objection by threatening to boycott the wedding service. If you have decided that your religious (or non-religious) wedding is important to you, then you cannot let your parents blackmail you by their threats. But neither should you engage in screaming matches with them, thereby allowing them to punish you emotionally for making the wrong choice of spouse and religion.

A word about angry exchanges with parents and other relatives: A few episodes of anger are healthy when a parent is threatening to boycott a wedding or being otherwise seriously out of line, but after a few angry conversations, why stay on that path? Instead, we suggest you call a meeting of the four of you—major conversations like this should involve both parents and both members of the couple—and calmly tell your parents that you have listened to their concerns and know that this wedding is hard for them because it will be outside their faith. Then tell them that you will not be changing the wedding plans and that you hope that they will be able to find a way to participate. Say that you will make any reasonable accommodations that might help them get through it, including not participating actively in the ceremony. Then say that you will not be talking with them again about this matter and that they can let you know their final decision at a later date.

If they continue to say they will not attend the wedding, say that it's their choice; it will make you very sad, and you hope they will change their minds, but it's their choice. Let them cook on it for a time; there is a good chance that one of the parents feels less strongly than the other and will work on that parent to relent. At the end of the day, most parents get to their children's wedding—holding their noses perhaps, but they get there.

We have emphasized the challenges and hard parts of handling disagreements with your parents during the wedding planning. It can seem too hard to work through these issues carefully and constructively, and instead some couples cave in to their parents or else try to wrestle them to the ground on every issue. But the payoff from handling this challenging process well is that your bonds with your parents grow stronger, more adult-to-adult and less parent-to-child. The wedding becomes a joint accomplishment and source of pride. Even when these good outcomes do not all happen, you can marry with the sense that you kept your integrity along the way, that you were strong personally and pulled together as a couple, that you listened with compassion, compromised when you could, and stayed the course without rancor or self-doubt when your core principles were at stake. What better way to start your life's journey together?

CHAPTER SIX

DEALING WITH FRIENDS AND COMMUNITY

J eri was doing fine with her parents and in-laws; it was her bridesmaids who were driving her crazy.

It's just 4 months before my wedding and my bridesmaids have yet to travel to visit me, leaving me to plan this entire wedding on my own. They have made no mention of a bridal shower and one of them just said she can't get enough time away from work to show up until just when the rehearsal starts. I think they're being so selfish and I wish I didn't choose them to be in my wedding!

Jeri's posting on a bridal chat room produced a chorus of responses like this one: "I do know how you feel. My maid of honor was totally disinterested when I began wedding planning, and also bailed on my first and only wedding dress shopping appointment without calling." Another bride ended her story with the advice she received about how to handle the problem:

My bridesmaids have been non-existent since I asked them to be in the wedding. I have been so stressed because I felt like they should be doing more. They have not shown up for any dress shopping appointments or even call to say why not. So yesterday a coworker of mine suggested that I don't have any bridesmaids, just like Princess Di did.

For the record, Princess Di did have bridesmaids—and a lot of professional help for the planning. The advice flowing to non-royal brides takes three common forms: fire your attendants if they are not doing their job, don't make a fuss because you don't want to lose your friends, or confront them about their bad behavior. Rarely does anyone suggest that the bride herself may have contributed to the problem by not being clear about what she expects, by expecting too much of them, or by asking the wrong people to begin with.

In Jeri's case, it turned out that her maid of honor and her two bridesmaids, all college friends who now lived out of state, did not have a clue about what their job was. Jeri was the first one in her group of friends to get married and the first to learn about wedding planning. No one is born with the idea implanted in their brain that the maid of honor should plan the wedding shower. Or that bridesmaids should help the bride shop for her dress. Jeri was seething because her friends were not stepping up for tasks they did not know they had taken on. She was losing sleep while her friends thought everything was moving along nicely. This is lesson one for dealing with the bridal party: *Make your expectations clear from the beginning.* This does not mean that you give everyone a list of demands; it just means that you share what you are hoping they can do, and get their buy-in. Here is an example of what you might say:

> I'm thrilled that you can be my maid of honor. It's so exciting. I have been learning what the maid of honor traditionally does, so let's talk about what parts you think you can do. It would be great if you could go shopping with me a couple of times to help me find my dress. How would you feel about doing that? Good family friends are already asking if they can plan the bridal shower, but they understand that typically the maid of honor hosts it.

It's a big job, and you have lots of things going on in your life, so if you can't, I would fully understand and these family friends would love to host the shower.

The goal is that you would come out of this conversation with a common understanding of what your maid of honor will help with. If she hesitates on a part of it, you can give her clearance to not sign up for that task. For example, if you suspect that she may freak out over the idea of hosting a shower because she is socially shy, very disorganized, and lives out of town, then you can be prepared to let her off the hook in a gracious way.

WHEN PEOPLE DON'T FOLLOW THROUGH

Let's say that you are clear with your bridal party about your expectations, that you think you have a deal—and then someone does not follow through. This was Lynn's situation:

My wedding is two months away. My bridesmaids have not ordered their dresses despite having the information ten months ago. (The dresses take 6-8 weeks to be ordered, not including alteration time.) I have talked with them numerous times about having another role in the wedding if being a bridesmaid would be a financial or scheduling setback. They informed that it would not be a problem. Now that we are in March, they are giving me a hard time with the style of the dress and getting the dresses made/altered by another seamstress. They are also questioning decisions I have made and that were agreed upon by the bridal party months ago. I have tried to be accommodating; however, I feel that it is too late to make certain changes. My maid of honor is the only one who has been supportive and helpful. She feels I should step back and let them run out of time to order their dresses, which would mean they would lose their bridesmaids role. I also feel that they are trying to find a reason for me to cut them as bridesmaids. How do I address this situation without adding more stress?

Keep in mind that there are laws against strangling people in wedding parties! The first question is whether these bridesmaids know the deadline for ordering their dresses; if not, this would be the first matter to clarify. Second is whether they still want to be in the wedding party. This could be cleared up during a lunch or phone call. After a warm-up time of chitchat, you could say something like this: "The wedding is coming up really fast now and we are trying to pin down the details of the ceremony. I want to double check to make sure you are still okay with being in the wedding party." If she says with shocked voice, "Of course I am!" then you can follow up with something like this: "Then I really need you to order your dress this week, because we are running out of time." If she asks again whether the dress can be changed, you can reply that you have decided to stay with the original plan and the original seamstress. Ask her if she can live with that, and get a commitment for her to order her dress by a fixed deadline. One of the posted replies to Lynn had additional advice:

> Tell them that you are absolutely at the deadline point. If the dresses are ordered any later than THIS WEEK, they simply will not have their dresses in time. Tell them they must get you their measurements within 3 days or they're out. Sorry, but that's the case. Then submit the measurements to the dress shop yourself. Anyone who doesn't submit to those deadlines will just have to suck it up and get over it.

We suspect that if Lynn had been this straightforward beforehand she would not be facing this problem with her bridesmaids. It's hard to make what your friends might consider threats: "Meet the deadline or you're fired from my wedding!" An alternative, if you don't want to be so blunt, is to give no ultimatums but just let events unfold with their logical consequences. Your bridesmaid is an adult, and you have just had an adult conversation about what you need from her on a specific timeline. You gave her a chance to change her mind, and she did not. Just hope that she will follow through and be prepared for the possibility that she won't by having a plan like the following one.

Ask the bridal shop for a drop-dead point beyond which they will not guarantee a dress. Make sure your procrastinating bridesmaid knows the deadline, including an urgent message from you a week beforehand. If she misses that deadline, then let her know via a phone call that time has run out and that you would like to discuss another role she might play in your wedding. The key is that she has made the decision, not you, by not following through on her task. She is not being fired—she resigned, and is being reassigned. You will feel disappointed, and maybe hurt, but not abused and frantic.

In other cases, you might want to go an extra mile or two for a dear friend who you know does not have her act together enough to follow through, even though her heart is with you. This might be your best friend from eighth grade who is now an overwhelmed single mom whose electricity is nearly disconnected twice a year because she forgets to pay the bill. Giving her a six-month deadline and expecting her to follow through—well, maybe that's not realistic. Your choices are to not to invite her to be in your wedding party (because she can't afford it or won't get her act together on the dress), or to invite her and give her extra support. For example, you might arrange a lunch date with her near the bridal shop, with the understanding that the two of you will stop by afterwards for her to get measured for the dress. You can have some fun, she will be grateful, and you will feel relieved. You will not feel taken for granted, because it was your choice to make the extra effort for your friend.

This brings us to next lesson: *If someone is predictably not responsible, take this into account in your planning.* This might mean telling the groomsmen that their deadline is two months in advance of the tuxedo store's deadline, or the groom dropping by his friend's house with a tape measure. If these people mean enough to you that you want them in your wedding party, and if you know their limitations, then plan accordingly so that you are not stressed and angry as your wedding approaches. Or offer them another role in the wedding that only requires them to show up on the right day. We will return to this theme later in the book when we talk about worst-case scenarios and impossible people on your wedding day. Difficult "leopards" in your life will not change their spots just because it's your wedding, so you have to plan your strategy accordingly.

DILEMMAS, DILEMMAS: WHO'S IN YOUR WEDDING PARTY?

Let's back up to a decision you may have already made: who to invite to stand up for you. You already know the issues involved, but here is a summary:
- Who is closest to you?
- Who you want to share this special event with?
- Who can support you the best?
- Who do you owe an invitation because they are family?

- Who is expecting to be asked, whether you want to ask them or not?
- How many attendants does your partner want to have?
- Who can afford the expense?

No small set of factors in your decision! Then add in other complications: If you have two best friends, which will be your maid of honor or groomsman? If you have three dear friends from high school and four more from college, do you have seven in your wedding party, or three, or four? Or do you ask just a subset of each group, thereby excluding the others? Ah, the loyalty binds and the potential hurt feelings! A number of these issues came together for Rachel:

> My fiancé and I just got engaged. I am having a hard time trying to choose my two bridesmaids. I only have one sister so she will be my maid of honor, but I would like to keep it to three bridesmaids so it will match the number of attendants my fiancé is having. He will have his best friend as his best man and his two brothers as his attendants. Here are the three options I am thinking about for my two bridesmaids:
> a) Two high school friends (they do not like each other) and I do not consider us as close as we used to be; however I have known them the longest. b) Two friends from work who I am very close with and have known for 5 years; they were both with me the night I met my fiancé at a bar. c) My fiancé has two married brothers with wives who I really like but have only known for three years. I lean towards these two because they will be my family and I believe family is stronger than friends sometimes. I do not want to hurt my friends from high school's feelings. I don't think any of the others would be hurt because they wouldn't necessarily expect me to ask them. However, I

feel that at least one of the girls from high school does not have money to be in the wedding, and she would not be good at helping with the wedding as far as planning goes. I plan to involve everyone listed in this group somehow, but would like some other opinions.

Got it? Where is King Solomon when we need wisdom? But Rachel at least is not feeling a lot of pressure from other people; mostly she feels internal pressure to make a good, balanced decision. Jessica, on the other hand, feels squeezed by her aunt and cousin:

> I saw my relatives for Thanksgiving, and my Aunt and female cousin were somewhat distant with me. Here is the back story:
> When I announced my engagement about 4 months ago at a family party, my Aunt started saying stuff like "Oh, good, Laura (my cousin) has never been a bridesmaid before," I ignored it, and hoped she would forget, as Laura and I are not close AT ALL and I really do not want her in the wedding.
> Well this week I saw them and Laura was asking about my wedding. I told her some things about it and she got really passive aggressive, saying "Oh, aren't people going to get seasick? I know I probably will." (My wedding is on a 150 foot yacht, and it stays IN THE HARBOR. It would be IMPOSSIBLE to get seasick.). It wasn't just that, it was many other things too. See, Laura is kind of bitter as she was supposed to get married a year ago and her fiancé called the engagement off. She is also my only older female cousin, and she is ten years older than me, so I think she thinks it is not fair that I am marrying first.
> I do not want to have an issue with them, but I really do not want Laura in the wedding. She is very tacky, gets drunk everywhere and has tattoos all over her body. At

my other cousin's wedding three years ago she got drunk and slept with TWO of the groomsmen in a car parked outside the wedding! If she does that at my wedding, I can't stop her, but at least she won't be associated with my bridal party. Besides, I already have six bridesmaids (that are all really wonderful and not passive aggressive at all.) What do I do? I am afraid that not including her will make it worse though. Maybe I should suck it up and include her just so I do not create a rift within my family? Laura's mom is really my favorite aunt.

Thanks for any advice!

You can imagine the tenor of the advice Jessica received from her fellow brides. Here are two strong ones, the first from a mother of a bride:

Honestly, I wouldn't have her do a damn thing! Why should you feel forced to have a tattooed, slutty, drunk, distant cousin bully you into having her in the wedding? Screw that! This is YOUR wedding, not anyone else's and you may regret asking her to do anything if she behaves like that! Also guess what? If she gets seasick (supposedly) she doesn't have to come. No one should feel they have to do anything they don't want to, and I am a mother of the bride! Girls, don't do it if you don't want to! If you really love your aunt and feel REALLY badly about not having Laura in the wedding, then the only other option is having her do a reading...as long as you don't fear she will embarrass you. If so, forget it. Good Luck!

I agree with the post before me. Don't be guilted into having her in your wedding!!! It is your day and you should have it the way you want it! This is the one time that it is completely okay to be selfish. Do what YOU want, not what other people want!! Good luck!

While we agree that Jessica should not feel coerced into having her cousin in her bridal party, we think there are bigger issues at stake. As we mentioned before, too much advice to brides and grooms nowadays take an extreme individualistic approach reflected in the second post: Be selfish, do it your way, forget what other people want. Not even Princess Di could get away with that attitude. The last time we checked, a wedding involves at least one other person besides the bride. Once you accept the idea that the wedding is about the bride, the groom, their families, and their friends and community, then the decisions become more complex. It's wonderful for the bride to be the princess on her wedding day, but there are a lot of other people in the royal party.

So let's look more deeply at Jessica's situation. It's hard not to respond to another person's passive aggressive behavior without being passive aggressive oneself. Which is what Jessica is doing by trashing her cousin on the Internet. (She could have left out details like the number of groomsmen in the car.) Jessica would not be in this dilemma if she did not love her favorite aunt so much. It's her aunt she is afraid of displeasing, not her cousin. And it was her aunt, perhaps feeling sorry for her daughter, who first went too far by publicly promoting Laura for the wedding party. Jessica could honor her aunt by including Laura in the wedding, but clearly not as a bridesmaid. As it stands, Jessica's frantic worry over this decision probably stems more from her guilt about saying no than it does a realistic fear that the family will split apart. Not many families splinter over a bride's decision to not invite a not-very-close cousin to be in the bridal party. The greater risk comes from Jessica letting herself be tormented into not making a straightforward decision, and then lashing out to third parties about how much she loathes her cousin. We end the discussion of bridal parties with our next lesson: *If you let wedding party decisions get you completely riled up, it means you are not taking charge. Make a decision and move on; people will get over it if you do.*

DEALING WITH GUEST LIST HASSLES

In chapter three we discussed how to negotiate guest lists with your families. Here we touch on what happens when the agreement starts to break down later on. One common scenario is that the bride or groom or a parent "discovers" that they *must* invite people not on the original list, like cousins or former neighbors, and then unilaterally invites them. They present you not with a proposal, but with a fact.

Another common breakdown occurs when someone feels they cannot say "no" to an eager potential guest. Maybe it's a woman from the bride's church, who, upon learning of the forthcoming wedding, gushes forth with "Oh, I can't wait to see you as a bride walking down that aisle!" Every socially polite bone in your body wants to you say, "Oh, yes. I can't wait until you can see me in my gown. I do hope you can come to the wedding." You have just opened Pandora's Box because how will you say "no" to others in your church?

Ellen and Brian kept a lid on their own loose-lipped invitations to a wedding that was already stretching their budget, but they found out just before the invitations were to go out that Ellen's grandmother had invited everyone in her sewing circle. This would not only break the budget, but also expand the guest list beyond the size of the reception hall. What do you say to grandma?

These scenarios are common and vexing for couples and families planning a wedding. Guest lists are important because they combine three powerful ingredients: money, priorities, and equality. The money part is obvious. When people invite additional guests, someone has to pay, which is a big problem if that person has not been consulted. When the bride's family is paying for the wedding and the groom's family invites extra guests, the negative feelings can be strong and the memories long. It's not a good way to begin in-law relationships. As we discussed in chapter two, guest lists are ways that people express their priorities about who is important to them. But it's the equality issue that sometimes leads to breakdowns when one family feels that the other is getting more than their "fair share" of guests. Instead of re-opening the discussion of the size of the guest list, one of the parents starts inviting additional friends or family members—making it hard to reverse course and un-invite them.

As with most interpersonal problems in wedding planning, prevention is the best approach, followed by graceful ways out of dilemmas as soon as you spot them. Prevention can take the form of discussing everyone's expectations up front, and making sure that both families understand the principles or reasons behind decisions about the guest list; for example, the reception hall has a fixed number of seats or wedding costs are to be kept within a definite limit. Adding guests has repercussions that everyone should understand. It's not a potluck block party.

To prevent yourselves from being squeezed by enthusiastic friends or coworkers, it can be helpful to develop a "storyline" that you can easily pull out. Some brides and grooms tell eager people that they are having a fairly small wedding, or that with the size of their families, there won't be much room for coworkers. A good storyline for people in your religious congregation who invite themselves to the wedding could be: "It would be wonderful if you could be at the wedding, but we have so many friends here that if we started inviting some people, we would have to invite too many people." Most people understand and won't feel personally excluded if you are clear, gracious, and not embarrassed about the choices you have made.

What if you are feeling pushed hard by a relative to invite more people than originally planned for? You can return to the original reasons for the decision on the guest list: "If we invite your golfing buddies, Dad, we won't have room for them." Or "That would add a thousand dollars to the cost of the reception, and I don't want to ask Jack's parents to pay for that." If someone has already sprung a leak by extending a verbal invitation, you can ask which people they are going to take off their part of the guest list. In practice, of course, there is usually some fudge room with guest lists because of illness and last minute changes in people's schedules. But it's important to let freelance inviters in your family know that this is a wedding, not an open house, and that there has been a lot of good thought put into the guest list.

Weddings are that rare event in life where everyone dear to you and your families comes together in support and celebration. That's why people will spend money and time they don't have, to travel across the continent for a brief ceremony and a party. Bridesmaids will purchase dresses they will never wear again. Groomsmen will act like gentlemen and wear odd suits in order to support their friend. Older relatives will postpone hip replacement surgery so that they don't miss the festivities. Your new friend at work, whom you spend a lot of time with, will gladly play third fiddle behind distant relatives and old friends you don't see much anymore. It's a fleeting but exquisite moment when all the ships in the convoy of your life come together from across the seas to one harbor, the place where you wed and launch a new ship. This special band of people, so carefully chosen by you and your parents, will never come together again. Which makes it so sweet when you have done your job well of calling them to your side.

CHAPTER SEVEN
DEALING WITH IMPOSSIBLE PEOPLE

U nless your life has been unusually blessed, you have some people in your inner circle who are, let's say, quite difficult to deal with. One type specializes in making life hard for others; your wedding is just their latest opportunity. Others are not generally difficult, but a wedding brings out their worst side. Either way, these are people who insist on their way first, second, and last. The most trying situations involve family members; bridesmaids or vendors may be impossible to deal with, but they don't have the clout of family members.

PREDICTABLE IMPOSSIBLE PEOPLE

Many families have one of these: someone who insists on attracting attention during big family events. Worrying about what stunt they will pull can drive you to crazy for months before the wedding. In one family, it was Aunt Elsie, who had a reputation for fainting into the aisle in front of the bridal procession. "I was carried away with the beauty of it all," she announced later after being picked off the floor and carried to the back of the church. The same family also had Uncle Bob, who generally got drunk at big family events. At the last wedding he repeatedly slobbered on the bride as he kept returning to the line for the traditional "dollar dance."

Ann, the bride, had enough to fret about as her wedding approached without worrying about her Aunt Elsie and Uncle Bob. But they kept returning to her mind as "wild cards" who could not be controlled. She knew what they were capable of. Her fiancé, Rob, tried to reassure her that they would probably behave for the big event, but then again he had never seen these two in action. Ann's father was a bit defensive for his siblings, and found their antics more amusing than alarming; that, of course, is why they had gotten away with their misbehavior over the years. "How can we control my brother and sister?" he would ask.

Ann and Rob could think of only three options: not invite the Aunt and Uncle, lecture them beforehand about not misbehaving, or just hope for the best. By this point in the book, you can probably guess what we have to say about the first option. Singling out a family member for exclusion from a wedding is as a big political act with grave repercussions over many years. It's certainly not something for a bride and groom to decide on their own (except in the most extreme situations) without full agreement from parents and other core family members. (If Uncle Bob had smashed the cake at a previous wedding reception and then fought off seven police officers, then perhaps a ban on inviting him to events with alcohol would have widespread support in the family.) In the same way, how can you ban frail Aunt Elsie from her favorite niece's wedding? It won't work to say, "It's my wedding and I will invite whoever I want." That's true if you do the Justice of the Peace route in a small office; if you decide on a public wedding, you will pay dearly for excluding core family members without the support of other family members.

How about talking with them in advance and asking them to behave? Another non-starter. For one thing, Aunt

Elsie's spells just come upon her; she would be insulted by any suggestion that she can decide not to have one. If you tell her tell to control herself and not steal your show, she might decide to steal it anyway for spite. The same with Uncle Bob, who certainly does not see himself as having a drinking problem and believes he is the life of every party he attends.

Is the only option to hope for the best? After all, impossible family members often behave on a wedding day, or at least do not act their worst. But perhaps you can do more. Ann and Rob got good advice from a sister-in-law. With the support of their parents, they assigned a female cousin to shadow Aunt Elsie and a male friend to hang out with Uncle Bob during the festivities. The cousin sat next to Aunt Elsie during the ceremony and made sure the aunt was not sitting directly next to the aisle. The friend bird dogged Uncle Bob during the reception, keeping an eye on his drinking, getting him a privileged dance slot (only one) with the bride, and taking him outside a couple of times for some fresh air. Everything went smoothly.

Who knows whether things would have gone well anyway? The point is that the wedding couple had a plan to keep two difficult relatives in check, a plan that did not embarrass the relatives and that gave the couple some piece of mind as they planned and lived out their big day. The lesson: *Since most impossible people are predictable, plan accordingly rather than being surprised and outraged.*

WHEN IMPOSSIBLE PEOPLE ARE CREATIVE

At least Ann and Rob had advance warning about what their difficult relatives might do. Molly knew her grandmother was an outrageous character, but was stunned by what she pulled at the wedding. Here is Molly's post:

Day of my wedding, I had the time of my life because I made a promise to myself that…[when things] went wrong (which they did) I would fix them and move on. BUT, one thing that happened that I think is maybe bothering me. So it starts with dad going to fill up grandma's car an hour before we're supposed to leave. (She loaned the car to us the day before to run errands.) And he locks the keys in the car at a gas station. Well, with reason, everyone is freaking out. We call grandma (who lives 30 minutes away) to come over.

She has to wait for someone to bring her, so she can come with her spare keys, and when she arrives, she has the keys but not the alarm thingy to deactivate the alarm system that holds the car locked. After much deliberation, dad talks to the garage owner (a friend of ours), and gives him the keys, telling him that dad has called a tow truck. It's going to take an hour, but his daughter is getting married and he needs to go…Obviously the garage owner says he'll take care of it, and given that he's a good friend of ours, we trust that everything will be ok (even if some wedding paraphernalia, like the ceremony readings, grandpa's tie, and other things, were locked in there…I just figured it wasn't really necessary).

But then here comes grandma, and mentions that there's no way she's leaving her car on the garage. It could get stolen. Dad mentions that not only will it be ok, but if something happens to the car, he'll vouch for it (mind you, the car is under Dad's name, grandma has no credit, but she does pay for it). She says "no," the car is more important to her. At this time, DAD IS CRYING begging her to go, Mom is out of her mind, telling her that this would be a horrible thing since grandma was in the bridal march, and she said "Yes, that's a thing that I've seen at a lot of weddings, but I didn't think it would happen in this one, and the car is more important." At this time, I AM

SAYING, "Don't worry grandma, I understand," telling mom, "Don't worry, it'll be ok," and telling dad, "Don't worry I don't mind" in such a peaceful tone that even I am scaring myself. My grandma was willing to miss her 1st granddaughter's wedding ceremony and God knows what else, to make sure that her car was safe. Well, she arrives 2 hours later, during the end of the cocktail hour, telling me that oh, she got the car fixed...My face was permanently fixed in a smile that day. Even she couldn't ruin my day, and frankly I believed that I was fine about it...

Come the end of the night (after all is done, I am saying goodbye to guests) and dad and grandma are talking and dad motions me to come over. He says that it was his fault for everything, that if he didn't lock the keys in nothing would have occurred, and I am just reassuring that don't worry, everything went great, and then grandma starts telling me how horrible I've been that I haven't come talked to her, that when she arrived it was her that had to come "all the way to where I was" to say hi, and that I should be ashamed that "I haven't dignified her with time." Mind you, I had a 75 person wedding, I went through all the tables said hi personally, but didn't spend much time with everybody. Duh, it's a freaking wedding. THAT was when I burst. I told her that there were 75 people that I had to greet, and that EVERYONE came to me to say hi, I didn't go to anyone because it would have been impossible, and how dare she after she showed such disregard for the most important part of my wedding.

The irony was that I had planned to have both of my grandmas in the march, she and her oh so hated rival, my grandpa's wife, who I consider my grandma, since she's taken care of me, and she treats me like a granddaughter, always. Well, guess who was the only one that walked down the aisle? And when they were taking the formal pictures, the picture with all the grandparents, she wasn't there. But I was mad that after so many things that had happened, now grandma is making me upset for expecting that I would just forget all my guests and spend time with the woman whose car and her dog are her everything, who leads a nomad life, who has no friends, and who is in constant fights with her own daughters.... I thought I let it go...but it's impossible to make grandma change her mind about what happened. In her mind saving her car was the first priority, and then making sure that I knew she was mad was the second one. So yeah, I am disappointed. I am writing Christmas cards to everyone, and joining it with wedding gift thank you cards. But I can't bring myself to send her one, which leads me to believe that I am mad.

I know the resolution, just get over it, be the "bigger person" and move on, and believe me, I am trying. But it still hurts.

Does grandma sound like bit of a handful? The background for why she was treacherous at the wedding did not come out until the last part of Molly's story. Grandma is a loner, a nomad who fights with everyone in her life. She is centered on herself and regards other people's needs as secondary at best. Her car was the most important thing to her that day; she probably resented lending it in the first place. Her choices, once it became clear that it would be towed away, were to keep the car in her sight at all times, or attend the wedding and worry constantly about the car. If this is true, it might actually have been for the best that she ditched the wedding and most of the reception, because she might have tried to dominate the proceedings with her worries and moans about her car being stolen.

Of course, this is our outsider's view of what happened. Molly was bound to be disappointed, frustrated, and furious at her grandmother. Molly did a great job of staying focused on the ceremony, the reception, and the people who came. She was a calm presence in a sea of anxiety in her family. Her outburst at grandmother at the end of the evening was entirely understandable, given grandmother's audacity to claim she was offended by being ignored during the reception.

In truth, Molly's grandmother had probably controlled the family for many decades with this kind of behavior. That's why no one stood up to her except Molly. In a healthier family, if grandma were freaking about her car being stolen and considering missing the wedding, her son or daughter would tell her firmly, "Mother, you are coming to the wedding. The car will be fine. You are coming to the wedding if I have to drag you inside." If she objected some more, the son or daughter would add, "I will not let you do this to my daughter. Come."

This kind of response is no longer possible after years of everyone being cowed. Grandma has a blank check in this family to be as self-centered as she likes. The wedding was just the latest time to cash in. In reality, Molly could not have prevented her grandmother from grandstanding in some unexpected way; the car problem was just an opportunity for grandmother to improvise a way to make the wedding about her own needs. Her main complaint was that she had been ignored, something that had nothing to do with the car. This woman is a master at what she does, a powerful family member whom a mere granddaughter cannot expect to contain. (She also is a sad, lonely woman who probably suffers from a personality disorder and no doubt had terrible parenting as a child.)

Molly knows what she has to do: move on. This means not expecting an apology and not retaliating by refusing future contact with her grandmother. If Molly can develop insight in to what makes a person act like her grandmother did that day, and more awareness of how her whole family has collaborated in allowing grandmother to act this way, then maybe she can eventually not take what happened so personally. This is a tall order, we understand, but family life is a tall order. Of course, sometimes wedding events involving impossible family members become food for hilarious stories when you come to see them as akin to natural disasters, on the par with a Florida wedding cancelled twice by repeated hurricanes. At the time, tears; after ten years, tales of mirth and laughter. No one likes stories about weddings that went perfectly.

DEALING WITH THREATS OR ULTIMATUMS

We turn now to situations with less humor. Earlier we discussed parent threats to boycott a wedding over religious differences. Let's assume that you have talked at length with your parents about this, explaining your reasons for where you are getting married and seeing if any compromises can be worked out, such as the example we described earlier where a clergyman from one family's religion had a role in the ceremony in another religious setting, and everyone was satisfied.

Alan and Jeannette worked for this kind of compromise but had to face the fact that his parents would not budge. A lifelong Catholic who wanted to go along with his bride's wish to be married in her hometown Lutheran church (there were no Catholic churches in the town), Alan knew that his conservative Catholic parents would be upset at attending a wedding in a Protestant church. For his own part, Alan definitely wanted his marriage to be recognized and blessed by the Church. He checked out the Church's rules and learned that he could receive a dispensation from the local bishop to be married in a Protestant church by a Protestant minister. He readily pursued this option and informed his family that the wedding would be fully accepted by the Catholic Church.

His parents would have none of it. They rallied the rest of the family on their side, claiming that their son would be committing a grave sin, and so would they if they attended the wedding. (One of Alan's aunts wrote him a letter pointing out that Jesus loved him more than Martin Luther did, something that Alan had never doubted.) Alan understood that his parents were nervous because they had never entered a Protestant church in their entire lives. But here they were digging in their heels more firmly than their Church did.

There were other factors involved, as they always are when family members act in ways that seem irrational. Alan's parents did not know Jeannette, having met her only once when Alan brought her home for a visit during a vacation. They did not approve of his marrying a stranger from a different part of the country; the religion difference sealed their opposition. There are always things not said in family showdowns.

This kind of scenario has played out in countless families over the centuries since marriage-by-choice replaced arranged marriages in the many parts of the world. It's the story line of Romeo and Juliet and countless other plays and movies. For the most part, parents who threaten to boycott the wedding do relent in the end, accepting the inevitable out of fear they will lose their child if they don't bend. They almost always show up for the wedding and make the best of it. Often they throw themselves into the wedding and enjoy it, letting their doubts float away with the champagne bubbles. Or at least they put on a good public face in order to avoid embarrassment in front of their whole community.

But boycott talk is unnerving for the bride and groom planning a wedding, and a source of bewilderment and frustration for the other set of parents who are cooperating and compromising. You cannot prevent threats and ultimatums because you cannot control anyone else's behavior, but you can handle yourself in a way that keeps you moving forward and minimizes the damage. Here are some guidelines for dealing with parents or other key family members who threaten to stay away unless they get their way. (Later we address the special circumstances of divorced parents.)

- Try to understand what is behind the threat to boycott the wedding. In addition to stubbornness and a need to control, there are usually other things going on, such as fear of losing their child, of being disloyal to their religion, or of embarrassment in front of extended family and friends. The parent who says, "I will not come if you have your wedding in a field" is probably expressing fear of losing face in the community.

- Work on compromises that alleviate some of their fears while not undermining your own dreams for your wedding. Seeking a religious blessing is an example, or choosing an outdoor setting that your elderly relatives can get to without hiking for a half mile through tall grass.

- Once you feel you have made appropriate compromises, stay firm with your final decision. If you talk as if it is still up for negotiation, you will encourage continuing threats and arguments. Tell your parents that it's a done deal: the Lutheran church with Catholic approval, the outdoor grotto with the nearby reception hall as the rainy day backup. End of discussion. This gives everyone time to get their minds around the decision.

- Make sure others in your family know your reasons for the final decision, and what you did to accommodate your others' concerns. Alan realized that he did not talk with enough family members directly about what he had done to assure that the Church would accept his wedding; as a result, these relatives were left with his parents' inaccurate version. Don't put your parents down in these conversations; just explain your side.

- Be gracious when your parents or others drop the idea of boycotting your wedding. Don't rub it in. Don't try to get them to admit they were wrong and you were right. A big life lesson: *You cannot control what your family members feel about your decisions or your actions.* What you can expect of them is to stop nagging you about a decision you have already made, to cooperate in the planning, and to be reasonably gracious at the wedding. More than that you can hope for but not insist on; approval is a freely offered gift.

Sometimes boycott threats come to fruition. Alan's parents and family ended up staying away from the wedding, to his great sadness, to Jeannette's great anger, and to the in-law's worry and befuddlement. To their credit, Alan and Jeannette did not dwell on who was absent, but had a fine wedding. The big choice point came afterwards: how do you go on after your family has boycotted your wedding despite your good faith effort to make it work for them? Some families split apart at this point, with years passing before further contact. Each side waits for the other to apologize, with the son or daughter expecting the parents to see their error and beg forgiveness, and the parents awaiting the same remorse from the other side. The more time that passes, the more each side thinks the other desires the cut-off, creating further hurt feelings. ("He knows where to reach us, and he does not pick up the phone.") Often it's not until grandchildren come along that the momentum swings towards family connection.

Alan and Jeanette handled it better than that. After a cooling off period of a couple of months during which Alan and Jeannette settled in a new city, Alan called home and suggested that he and his wife come home for Thanksgiving. His parents were mightily relieved to break the ice. The Thanksgiving went well partly because no one talked about the wedding; no apologies were offered or requested. To her great credit, Jeannette did not harbor a well-deserved grudge at her in laws, and gave Alan the room to reconcile in his own way with his parents. She decided that her future children needed to know their grandparents, however obnoxious they had been over the wedding. In future years, Jeannette and Alan did produce the first grandchild in the family, to the grandparents' delight, and the wedding pain receded, although it never fully went away, especially for Jeanette. Alan's mother, always one to conveniently forget about upsetting things, eventually looked at the wedding pictures with delight, as if she had been there and remembered that wonderful event. Lesson: *Even the worst wedding behavior can be forgiven if you want to remain a family.*

WHEN DIVORCED PARENTS BECOME IMPOSSIBLE

With divorced parents, the threat to boycott the wedding can be more poisonous than in Alan and Jeanette's situation where they were dealing with limitations of both parents, but not being pulled between the parents. In one sadly common situation, the divorced father angrily said he would not show up if the bride's mother came to the wedding; she had recently remarried and the father knew that her new husband would be accompanying her. The bride tried to problem solve this with him, suggesting that the parents sit on opposite sides of the church and the banquet room. The mother was willing to accommodate in this way, but the father would not bend: it was either he or his "ex," but not both. The bride went through tears, rage, and screams at him, begging him to relent, but he would not budge. Then he showed up at the last minute at the church and slipped into a pew. The bride did not know whether she was more furious at him for this earlier ultimatum or for showing up and startling her at the last minute just before she walked down the aisle with the groom (she had hoped to walk with her father).

This bride could not control her father's actions, but perhaps she could have handled herself differently so as not to feel so victimized by him. Here is a conversation that might have left her feeling that she had maintained her dignity:

> Father: I tell you I won't come if she does.
> Daughter: As I've told you, that makes me feel very sad and angry.
> Father: What about my feelings?
> Daughter: Dad, this is an occasion when I expect you to put your own feelings aside for one day—for me.
> Father: Honey, I'd like to but I can't. I know I can't face her.
> Daughter: I don't believe that, but I realize you do. I want you to know that I would not in a million years choose between my parents like you are asking me to do. If Mom asked me to not invite you, and threatened to boycott if you came, I would tell her the same thing. You are both invited and the decision is yours about whether you come. And I won't discuss my decision any further. Mom has accepted my invitation and is coming to the wedding, and you will have to decide whether you are coming.
> Father: I'm not trying to hurt you, but I don't think I can handle it.

Daughter: It's your choice. I just ask that you let me know your final decision a week before the wedding because I have to make plans.

This clearly would be a delicate conversation, one that would take considerable rehearsal. Even if not done perfectly according to "script," the key would be for her to put the burden of the decision back on her father. It's not the two-way decision he is trying to make it out to be, namely, that she is choosing to reject her father by including her mother. She has invited her mother and father. Her mother has accepted; now it's up to him to make his own decision. Some things are not worthy of negotiation, and anyone who asks you to negotiate with them is manipulating you and avoiding personal responsibility.

When people close to you make unreasonable demands and threats, it's tempting to respond by either wimping out ("Have it your way') or blowing up ("I hate you; go to hell"). Brides and groom often alternate between the two. Giving in (as opposed to compromising) leaves you feeling empty about your wedding and resentful towards the people who manipulated or bullied you. But engaging in screaming matches is also ineffective and punishes you along with them. During temper outbursts, most of us say things we regret, and the decisions we are defending don't appear at those moments to be those of mature adults. Bridal chat rooms are filled with verbal outbursts such as: "It's my wedding, damn it, and I don't give a hoot what anyone else thinks. They can all stay home...." This is meltdown language, understandable given the pressure but best avoided during serious negotiations with people who are part of the wedding.

"Impossible," of course, is in the eye of the beholder. We have reserved the term here for people who will neither support your decisions nor work with you to find common ground, or who have personal problems that make clear communication not feasible. If these people are family members and therefore part of your life in the future, then the trick is to develop a plan to deal with them in a way that does the least damage to them, you, and your wedding. Going to war with family members usually ends with too many casualties; it's better to think in terms of managing the situation than of winning a victory. If a small compromise helps an impossible family member feel vindicated and then behave better, so much the better. You don't have to see it as caving in to their demands so much as giving them a graceful way out of a mess they have created. Thus you will demonstrate to your whole family that you can maintain your integrity in the face of people whose style is to bend people to their own will. Remember: you cannot change difficult, self-centered family members, so try not to agonize about winning their approval. They may continue to be impossible, especially on stressful occasions that bring out the worst in all of us, but you will be a puzzle for them: someone who stands up for yourself without losing contact with them. Come to think of it, that's the art of being in a family.

CHAPTER 8

WHEN BAD THINGS HAPPEN BEFORE THE WEDDING

After September 11, 2001 there were many stories of weddings held or postponed. Everyone could understand the couples' dilemma. Do you go ahead with a long-planned wedding when your relatives and friends are in shock and mourning, and when travel is impossible? The same scenario occurred throughout Florida during the hurricanes in 2004; obviously you don't have your wedding when conditions outside are life threatening, but what if it is scheduled for two days later when everyone is still digging out? Families go through deaths just before weddings, couples have relationship emergencies during their engagement, and sometimes the reception hall burns down a week before. We will skip the facility fire (you are on your own for that one), and instead start with bad things that happen in couple relationships that can lead to postponing or even canceling the wedding.

BAD THINGS IN THE COUPLE RELATIONSHIP

Here's a nightmare that every bride (or groom) would dread writing about in a chat room:

> I found out that my fiancé recently posted a personal ad online for a "no strings attached encounter" with someone.

It said, "If you are a mature, sensual woman, I would love to take you out tonight...."

I am freaking out. My heart is totally shattered. We just bought a house together and I think since I'm not living there yet, he advertised the posting in that city—he was going to bring someone to our house! Our bed!

We have had an amazing, incredible relationship for three and a half years. The bedroom stuff is amazing, we're best friends, both completely attracted to each other. I don't get it! This is totally out of the blue—and SO unlike him! He's never as much as looked at another girl while we've been together. And no, I'm not naive or oblivious.

Do you think he's just trying to have a fling before we get married? Even so, I think this is completely unacceptable. I'm so lost—this is a deal breaker in my mind, but my heart doesn't want it to end. I'm heartbroken. Should I try to fix this and move on, or should this be the end?

What a shattering discovery. It not only throws her future upside down, but it also makes her question her judgment over the past three-plus years. Nearly everyone would agree that she should not proceed with the wedding planning and that she must confront her fiancé. The trickier judgment call is whether she would then walk away and never turn back, or whether she should see if he and the relationship are salvageable. We certainly cannot pretend to know what the right decision for her is, and we have only a snippet of information about their relationship—all of it good except for this one whopper of an offense.

One question for the bride to ask herself (or the groom if the roles were reversed) is whether she could imagine emotionally getting over this betrayal. If she knows herself well enough to see that she would always hold a grudge or feel insecure and mistrustful, no matter what he does or says in the future, then this would be a good reason to say goodbye and look for a new mate. On the other hand, if she holds out some possibility that she could put this behind her, depending on how he and she handle this crisis, then she might benefit from the some ideas for how to proceed. The following suggested guidelines can be viewed as a series of red lights and yellow lights: if he responds in one way, stop and go no farther; if he responds in a second way, proceed with caution. And if she does not believe him at any point, that's a final exit sign.

Step One: Confront him with the email. Do it face to face at his place rather than on the phone. Simply put the email in front of him, with no comments, and wait for his reaction. People tend to show their true selves when surprised like this. If he responds with one of the following copouts, have your exit speech prepared, deliver it, and walk out the door.

- The counterattack: "Where did you get this? Why were you in my email?" This may be the worst possible response, turning defensiveness into hostility. Consider yourself fortunate that you discovered your man's true colors before you married him.
- The lie: "I don't know who wrote this message. It wasn't me?" In the highly unlikely scenario where this was true, he would know that, say, his teenage nephew had gotten into his email account, and you could both check out the story. Just saying, "It wasn't me!" is immature and a big red light.
- The dismissal: "What's the big deal? I was just having some fun on the Internet. You know I would never follow through." Many misguided married men and women nowadays who have Internet affairs and claim

it's all harmless. You don't want to marry someone with that attitude.

- The easy apology: "I am so sorry. I don't know what got into me. It will never happen again. I hope we can move on." This person does not get the depth of what he did, instead giving a response appropriate to forgetting to pick you up after work. Let him know that you are not prepared to just "move on" and that there is a lot more to be talked about.

- The feel-sorry-for-me ploy: "I am such a terrible person for doing this to you. You must hate me. I will kill myself if you leave me over this." Any response that invites you to immediately feel badly for him is a manipulation. Tell him he is responsible for his own life, and head for the door.

- A proceed-with-caution response: "What I did was terrible. I am so sorry to hurt you this way. I will do anything to work this out with you." However he says it, the message is that he accepts responsibility for the betrayal, feels terrible about what he has done to you, and wants to keep talking. If your gut tells you he is being honest, then you can decide to go to the next step in the conversation.

Step Two: Ask him to tell you the full, unvarnished story. The next red light is any lying, such as telling you this was the only time he ever did this stupid thing. The odds are nearly perfect that this is not the first time he has solicited sex via email, or at least engaged in sexual relationships over the Internet. Tell him directly that you don't believe him and that if he continues to not tell you the whole truth, your relationship is over. Tell him you do not want him to protect you from the truth, and that you want the whole story: when he started these contacts on the Internet, how often he has met women for sex, what lies he has told to cover it up, and whether he had planned to continue his infidelities after the marriage.

This will be terribly painful for you, which is why you should give yourself permission to not have this conversation and simply walk out of the relationship. But if you want a chance to salvage it, the two of you have no choice but to put everything on the table. (This is what marriage therapists have learned that couples need to do to recover from affairs.) Since the offending partner understandably is afraid to tell the whole story, remind him that everything now depends on his complete honesty, because otherwise you will not be able to trust him again. If he gets defensive and tries to put it back on you ("Why should I bare my soul if you are not going to believe me anyway"), that's a red light. Do not defend yourself for making him uncomfortable. Tell him again that he has no choice but to level with you if he wants any hope of you taking him back.

Trust your gut here about whether he is telling you the truth about his history with other women during your courtship and engagement. If you feel that he is leveling with you, then you have to decide whether you want to try to forgive him and restore trust. Here are two examples of scenarios that might lead you to either end the relationship or keep going forward.

- Final red light: He has cheated on you with many women since the beginning of your relationship, told many lies, and put your health at risk with unsafe sex with anonymous women. This guy has serious psychological problems and is able to fool you completely. How could you ever feel safe again with him?

- Another yellow light: He has a history of using Internet flirtations for titillation and masturbation but has never followed through to meet the women. We are not excusing his behavior in any way, but this scenario (if it is the truth) suggests he is more salvageable as a future husband than in the first scenario. Many marriages face this kind Internet infidelity and get through the crisis. Of course, if he has met some women for sex, this complicates your decision about whether to end the relationship or go to the next step.

Step Three. Ask him to start therapy for himself and your relationship. A big mistake is to try to forgive and forget after an emotional tears-and-anger conversation that ends with a false reconciliation and both of you in bed together. Someone who has a pattern of betrayal has a responsibility to dig into the underlying reasons and to learn how to behave with greater health and accountability in the future. It's not enough to say, "I'm sorry, this was a wake up call, and I won't ever do it again" (like professional athletes who beat up fans in the seats). That may work for a one-time infraction, such as a drunken groom who behaves inappropriately with a stripper at his bachelor party. A groom (or bride) who is unfaithful during an engagement has deeper problems to confront. And the couple has problems they need help with together. So ask him if he is willing to go to therapy with you. If he balks, that's a danger sign that he is not yet taking this problem seriously. Tell him that this is part of the deal for deciding if you want a future with him. If he keeps saying things like "I don't believe in shrinks," or "We can handle our problems ourselves," this suggests that your fiancé may not have the courage or the psychological resources to face himself. Ask him to think about it. If a week or so goes by and he has not changed his mind about getting help with you, then that might be a final red light.

Of course there might be another whole set of explanations for the fiancé's betrayal on the Internet. He might have been looking for a way out of the engagement by "accidentally" allowing is fiancée access to the incriminating email. People have strange ways of saying they no longer want to get married or stay married; sometimes it's by acting badly and forcing the other person's hand. Another explanation might be a call for help from a guy who feels out of control of his sexual impulses. By setting up a circumstance where his fiancée discovers his problem and confronts him, he might be saying he wants help. In that case, he would leap at the idea of therapy, or suggest it before his fiancée does.

We hope you never face this kind of problem—now or during your marriage. But perhaps our analysis and guidelines might be useful if you do, or helpful when you advise friends who face this problem. Many of these ideas apply to other common couple emergencies that come up during engagements (and marriages), such as what happened to another couple, Sabrina and David. They had never had a major argument until a couple of months into their engagement, after they started to live together. David was a big guy, a former football player and now a coach. Aggressive in the sports world, he was normally laid back with Sabrina and his friends. But you never really know someone until you have a major argument with them.

One night Sabrina and David got into a big argument about how much time he spent away from home being a coach (if he was not with his players, he was reviewing tapes of opponents' games or on the road recruiting). He tried to reassure Sabrina that this was a bad season and that things would lighten up, but she would not be comforted. Now that they were living together and she depended on him for companionship, she was beginning to understand his lifestyle, and she was worried about their future. When they had these conversations before, David always remained calm. This time he blew up in a way that scared Sabrina. He jumped off the sofa and yelled that she was acting like a bitch. When she told him to never call her that name, he threw a lamp across to the other side of the room. When she screamed that he was acting like a crazy man, he came across the room, told her to stop shouting, and grabbed her by her arms in a tight grip, nearly bruising her because of his strength. When she shouted at him to take his hands off her, he threw her onto the sofa and charged out of the house. A sobbing Sabrina called her mother and told her what happened. An hour later, David returned and tearfully apologized, saying that he would never do something like this again. A couple of days later, Sabrina told him that she wanted to postpone the wedding because he had scared her so much.

A very upsetting and confusing experience during an engagement, especially because it was so unexpected. Many of the same principles apply there that we discussed in the infidelity story. Sabrina was right to take this episode very seriously. Most couples have verbally loud arguments, but David crossed the line when threw the lamp, grabbed and held Sabrina, and then threw her on the sofa. It does not matter that he did not slap or punch her; he acted in a physically violent and threatening way, and she had every right to feel alarmed. She also did the right thing by calling someone immediately and telling the story, as opposed to keeping it a secret, and by putting a stop to the engagement until she could sort things out.

Once again, Sabrina understandably might decide to end the relationship entirely. She has to sort out for herself whether she can ever trust him again during an argument. But if she wants to try to salvage the relationship, and if this was indeed the first time he had ever scared her, then she needs a plan of action similar to the one we outlined earlier. In this case, David had already apologized, which is a good first step. But there must be more if he is to win back Sabrina's trust. First of all, he should accept full responsibility for his physical outburst and not try to pin some of the blame on Sabrina. No doubt she had a part in escalating the argument, but the person who is violent is fully responsible for the shift from angry words to physical deeds. As all professionals who work with domestic violence know, no one's words make someone else turn violent.

He should also be willing to talk about his temper, something she had not seen before. No man treats his fiancée this way unless he has a problem with anger. Claiming that it was one-time lapse is not enough, just as a first affair cannot be dismissed as a one-time lapse. Promises to never lose his temper again are empty unless he understands why he loses his temper and what he can do differently. Even the most abusive people are only abusive once in a while; the problem is that they don't know enough about what triggers them and how they respond in a healthier way.

It comes down again to David being willing to seek therapy with Sabrina. In some ways, it's better that this episode happened before they got married, because they now have time to sort out what happened and what they can do about it. Postponing the wedding, though, is an important way for Sabrina to signal that things are not business-as-usual, kiss-and-make-up. People can make bad mistakes one time, for which they can be forgiven if they take responsibility and work on change. Getting away with a repeat performance signals that it's okay to be abusive. That's why many therapists treating this couple would suggest that Sabrina lay down a firm ground rule for the future: if he ever touches her again in anger, she will leave forthwith and never return. Zero tolerance for repeat offenses.

WHEN BAD THINGS HAPPEN IN THE FAMILY

Let's move past bad behavior by a fiancé(e) to situations when wedding plans are threatened by upsetting family events. The most common big one is the death of a parent, sibling, or grandparent. The first story is one in which the death occurred well before the wedding but its effects lingered. Seth's dad passed away unexpectedly soon after he and Trish got engaged. They were both in graduate school finishing their last intense summer session, after which Seth was going to start a Ph.D. program without any time off. Seth was an only child and lived on the east coast. His dad, divorced from Seth's mother and living on a different coast, left Seth to sort out the entire estate, including complicated property and professional issues. Never close to his father but now dealing with grief and the burden of settling his father's affairs, Seth became very depressed and told Trish that he did not have the emotional energy to talk about the wedding plans. Not wanting to pressure her fiancé, Trish turned to her maid of honor, Heather, for advice and support. Heather became increasingly worried for this couple. The last thing a couple should do, Heather thought, was to go through wedding planning with only one emotionally healthy partner, and then have a wedding in which only one spouse was there in spirit. Heather took a big risk by asking Trish if she would consider postponing the wedding until Seth was in a better emotional place and the two of them were settled in their new city. Instead of being shocked at the suggestion, Trish took it in, and brought it up to Seth. The couple decided to postpone the wedding a full year, scheduling a weekend getaway on the original date they would have gotten married. They knew it was best decision they could have made, and they had no regrets. Seth was fully present on his wedding day, and his extended family was able to celebrate Seth's father's life and memory at the wedding. This was a brave couple who made the hard decision to postpone their wedding.

At least Seth and Trish had plenty of time to make their decision. It's much harder when a close family member dies just before the wedding, and worse still when the death is sudden and unexpected. It's a bridal couple's nightmare to think that they or the people close to them will have to choose between a wedding and a funeral—between celebrating the start of a new life together and mourning the loss of a loved one. How do you decide whether to go on with the wedding or to postpone it? Obviously the decision is influenced by who died and how close the death is to the wedding. Let's assume the worst-case scenario in which the death occurs during the week prior to the wedding, with the family thrust into simultaneous funeral and wedding planning. We don't know any existing guidelines for this kind of thing, and the personal and financial implications are serious. We will just offer our own best thinking in the form of questions to think about.

- What would the deceased person have wanted? Sometimes a sick, elderly grandparent has already told the family to go ahead with the wedding no matter what. A funeral can be postponed more easily than a wedding, and a wedding is about the future in a way that a funeral is about celebrating a past life. Olympic athletes sometimes use this principal to decide whether to come home for a funeral or to compete: what would my family member have wanted me to do?

- Is a key person in the wedding so devastated that he or she could not go through with it? Clearly if the groom is beside himself at the sudden loss of his brother in an accident, and is thoroughly depressed during the days afterwards, then it might be best for the bride to suggest postponing the wedding. Let him be the one to say, "No, let's go ahead." If the bride's father has died and her mother is in a dark depression and obsessed with how she will survive as a widow, then the couple might offer to postpone the wedding. Sometimes this offer alone makes the grieving family member feel supported enough to rally and make a go of the wedding.

- How long can you postpone making a final decision? If you can wait until after the initial shock of the death has subsided, you may make a better decision. For example, the final deadline might be when out-of-town guests will begin their travels. Buying time can allow the couple to sort through their own feelings and to consult others.

- How do the people who are paying for the wedding feel about proceeding versus postponing? There can be substantial losses here, and the wishes of the ones taking those losses should count in the decision— not necessarily trumping everyone else's feelings, but important to be heard and respected. This can be especially dicey if the death was in the groom's family and the bride's parents are footing the wedding bill.

- How do other key family members feel about going ahead with the wedding? If everyone is united on a decision to proceed, then you are on safe ground. If there is disagreement or indecisiveness, then you have a real problem. We turn next to this awful scenario.

What can you do if it appears that key family members

feel differently about postponing the wedding in the face of a death in the family? What follows is just our view; others might take a different approach. We suggest that you first decide who is in the core group you want on board for the decision. This might be your parents (unless one of your divorced parents has not been a major player in your life and the wedding), the living grandparent if the loss was to that person's spouse, and the siblings you are close to and trust. (A sibling who had been disconnected from you and your wedding might not qualify for the inner circle of decision making.) You would bring these people together in the same room if at all possible.

It's best to approach this kind of meeting with a clear idea of what it will take to make the final decision. You could decide that you are going to listen to everyone's feelings and ideas, and then go away and make the final decision based on how you weigh the options. We suggest a different approach: that you decide in advance that you will only go ahead with the wedding if there is full consensus, with everyone buying in, that you should do so. If a core family member is strongly against holding the wedding as planned, then we think it may be best to call it off. Sometimes they won't say it directly, but say, for example, that the bride's widowed mother keeps whispering, "I don't know if I can go through with the wedding," we think it's best to postpone the wedding and put your efforts into supporting her and the family during the funeral. Why? Because it's better to be loyal to a deeply distressed loved one than to insist on your original plans. Money and convenience aside (no small matters, we agree), you can get married any time you want. Death and loss have their own timetable. Imagine yourself at your mother's own deathbed in the future: will you feel better having offered her extraordinary support and self-sacrifice at a crisis time in her life, or having plunged ahead with your wedding as planned? As we said earlier, there is also a good chance that your act of generosity will be met with an equally generous insistence to proceed with the wedding.

WHEN A NATURAL DISASTER STRIKES

Natural disasters like weather storms are not as bad as family deaths but they are more likely to happen to your wedding. There are logistical nightmares such as when the bakery vehicle cannot get the cake to the reception or the clergyperson cannot get out of his or her driveway in the snowstorm. Our focus here is on making decisions with the interests of everyone in mind. When natural disasters occur, everyone is affected: local people because they are stuck at home or need to attend to their own damaged property, and out-of-town people because they will have trouble traveling to the wedding. If the travelers arrive and you postpone the wedding, they may have just spent a load of money for airplanes, gowns, and hotels—and then you will be asking them to turn around and come back for a repeat set of expenses! The local people may be just as annoyed if you go ahead, putting them in a bind of feeling disloyal if they fail to show up, but resentful that they are expected to put your wedding over their own safety of household security.

Again, no right and wrong answers; each situation is unique. The key guidelines are to consult with people you trust and then communicate to everyone the reasons for your decision and your understanding of how it affected them. Most guests (but not the impossible ones!) will understand and accept your final decision if you make it responsibly and have empathy for their situation. For example, if you have lots of out-of-town guests already in place when a big storm knocks down half the trees in your city and leaves many of your hometown guests with big snowdrifts and no electricity, you might decide to proceed with a makeshift wedding (by candle light in a cold church) because it will be very difficult to assemble your out of town guests again. You can recruit help for telephoning your local guests to let them know the wedding is on but that you will understand if they cannot make it. Then have a party later on for the locals. Of course if the person performing the wedding can't make it.... but what a great story in the future!

Brides are famous for freaking out when bad things happen near their wedding day, and many grooms are not far behind. One of the nice ironies of wedding planning is that if you pay attention to how others in your family and community are affected when bad things happen before your wedding—instead of only worrying about how it affects you—then they are likely to come through with loads of good will and good ideas for how to solve the problem. Weddings are real life exaggerated. The bad things are worse because everything is more intense, but the good things far outshine the bad when you keep your balance and stay close to the people who love you.

CHAPTER 9

LET'S ALL GATHER FOR A WEDDING

U p till now you've been able to manage challenging people one-to-one. You sat down with your father or your maid of honor, but now the whole cast of characters is gathering together and interacting with one another. Once your families and other guests begin to assemble for your wedding, they play off each other in unexpected ways. Whatever illusions you may have had that you are in charge of this whole wedding thing now vanish. But we have ideas that may help you cope with the unexpected, keep your perspective, help your guests enjoy themselves, and turn surprises into delights.

THE GATHERING OF THE CLANS

Ideally people in each of your families will look forward to getting to know the other family. Although your parents may feel that way, most other family members are focused on their own relatives and family friends, some of whom they have not seen for years. They come out of family duty, hopefully a pleasant one, and not to get to know strangers. They prefer to cluster among themselves and to observe with curiosity, and sometimes amazement and concern, the gaggle of new relatives-by-marriage. If you did not appreciate this truth before, you now know that every marriage is a mixed marriage, a coming together of two cultures.

Your people, it turns out, have strange tribal customs for big events such as weddings. This can be as basic as how on-script versus spontaneous a wedding should be. You have carefully planned the order of formal toasts during the reception, but the groom's uncles take over with their own roast of the groom. The bride grits her teeth throughout, and is annoyed that her groom is grinning with delight. The groom's relatives note to one another how uptight the bride's kin folk seem to be—hey, it's a wedding, for crying out loud, not a funeral! Which is precisely the point that the bride's family are troubled about—it's a wedding, not a hoedown.

The Smith family had a unique wedding tradition that the bride had mentioned only in passing to her groom: the new spouse was inducted into the clan by the placement of a colander (objects generally used for straining spaghetti) over his or her head during the groom's dinner. This coronation is performed by Uncle Marv and a court of other relatives all wearing colanders bestowed at previous family weddings. It's how you get into the Smith family, and of course you are expected to appreciate the humor: it's a quirky twist on the typical wedding trappings of china and crystal. For the Smiths, it's a moment for frivolity in the midst of formality.

Guess what? The groom's family was not amused by the surprise coronation during *their* groom's dinner. They seemed even more annoyed because the colander routine was obviously the highlight of the evening for many people at the dinner. For his part, the groom tolerated the moment, wishing his bride had better prepared him and wondering what his parents thought of it all. Lesson: *Prepare your families for the quirks and odd customs of the other family.*

MANAGING LAST-MINUTE PEOPLE PROBLEMS

Erin's sister and maid of honor, Chloe, turned into the sister-from-hell on the day of Erin's wedding. Reasonably cooperative during the wedding planning, Chloe had stuffed her feelings about her young sister getting married when she herself had no immediate prospects. Come the wedding day, though, she fussed as if she were a panicky bride. She woke up with the disastrous pimple on her cheek. Her dress did not fit right—she could not have gained weight—and how could she look like this for the pictures? The original hairdresser was ill and the new one completely ruined the hairdo, and her makeup was atrocious. Finally ready to take her part in the reception, she discovered that her heels now made her taller than the best man! Chloe offered her sister, the bride, not one bit of support that day.

Erin was flummoxed and distracted by Chloe's behavior. She found herself continually trying to calm and reassure her sister, meanwhile doing a slow burn of resentment. But there was more going on here than Chloe's self-centered behavior. Their mother was falling all over Chloe with concern and support, taking every complaint with great seriousness. Poor Chloe, she's having such a hard time. The mother was playing her part in a longstanding family drama: Erin had long ago been cast as the strong, capable daughter who did not need her mother very much, whereas Chloe was the more emotional, vulnerable daughter who required mother's worried attention. Put everyone under the stress of a wedding day, add in Chloe's unspoken feeling of envy, and you have the makings of a wedding day challenge for Erin. If mother was not playing along, she could have taken Chloe aside and told her firmly to shape up and stop whining because this is her big sister's wedding day. Either Chloe would have complied or everyone would have ignored her; in either case, Erin would have had the center stage attention she deserved. A family systems lesson: *It takes a least three people to make a problem really bad at a wedding or any other time.*

All you can do in Erin's situation is to apply a core message of this book: *Keep your balance and don't try to control the feelings and reactions of other people.* Of course Erin can try in small ways to calm down her sister and remind her that she herself is also feeling stressed. But Erin telling Chloe to stop acting like a self-centered brat would only produce a tidal wave of tears and recriminations about how much Chloe has done for this wedding and how little she has been thanked and appreciated. Mom would then intervene on behalf of her duckling daughter, and a nuclear meltdown would commence unless someone stepped in. A better approach, if you can muster it, is to see your sister's performance as a piece of unexpected bad weather on your wedding day, unfortunate and distracting but not worth too much of your attention. You might also ask a trusted bridesmaid to discretely baby-sit your sister until you are safely away after the festivities.

In future weeks and months you have time to reflect on what your sister did on your wedding day, and allow yourself to feel justifiably angry. But if this was just a small part of an otherwise glorious experience, it doesn't have to preoccupy you unless you let it. If you can muster enough perspective, you can try to understand what happened in a deeper ways than just concluding that your sister is a selfish, self-centered person who tried to ruin your wedding day. It is likely that she did not wake up that morning with the deliberate intent of sabotaging you. And like most of us, she is more self-focused when under stress and when dealing with painful feelings she can't talk about or maybe even acknowledge to herself. The other side of the truth about family members who grandstand during a wedding is that they are fragile people who feel diminished when others are the center of everyone's love and attention. It's as if there is only a limited amount of emotional food to go around; your abundance means less for her, or it reminds her how little she feels she has received in the past. If she were an old high school friend that you made the mistake of putting in the bridal party, you could move her out of your life circle. But Chloe is your sister; she is family and thus in your life circle whether you like it or not. She will be an aunt to your children, someone you celebrate many holidays and life milestones with. If she marries, you will be her matron of honor—and do a better job than she did because you are a different person. So it's best to forgive her now even though she may never apologize—and to be prepared for this leopard to keep her spots in the future.

THE RECEPTION: WHEN YOU LOSE CONTROL OF EVENTS

During most wedding ceremonies, the guests are spectators at a carefully crafted ritual. The reception afterwards is a different matter. You plan the overall flow of the event, but your guests also shape it to their wishes. This is when non-family members do their thing and have their say. It's like the point we made about bachelor and bachelorette parties: once you agree to have them, you can't dictate what will happen, although you can control your reactions to what happens.

During the wedding reception, couples who have been elevated and celebrated by their community are often teased and toyed with. After honoring the bride and groom with gifts and special attention, guests at traditional wedding receptions put the couple through embarrassing ordeals such as removing and tossing a garter, being the object of playfully mocking humor (especially the groom), having to kiss whenever the guests tinkle their glasses (another Midwest custom), and enduring practical jokes as they prepare to leave for their honeymoon. Embarrassment rituals occur in many cultures, such as in Hindu weddings where the couple are required to play various games for the benefit of the guests. It is as if the community wants to bring the couple back to reality and remind them that in the future they will not be more any more special than those who know and love them the best.

In truth, some rituals you can avoid, such as by the bride not wearing a garter and informing her wedding party as such. Others you cannot avoid, but you can play with your guests' expectations. Anticipating the local tradition of having to stand and kiss each time the guests clink their glasses in unison, Patrick and Lea Anne went along the first two times. The third time, they arranged for the groom to kiss the matron of honor and the bride to kiss the best man. The audience was set back on its heels. Having tweaked the traditional ritual in this way, the couple proceeded to kiss with good humor throughout the rest of the evening whenever glasses tinkled their glasses, which happened less frequently than usual because the guests were not sure what would happen next! The bride and groom had let their guests know that they were voluntarily cooperating in the spirit of fun, but were willing to poke back.

Our advice for relating to your guests during the reception: *Do your best planning for the reception but then keep your good humor and go with the flow of what your community does with you.* It's their time to help shape your wedding.

HELPING GUESTS ENJOY THEMSELVES

We said at the outset of the book that we are writing about the people in weddings, not the logistics. But logistics help the people feel part of the community celebration of your wedding. At the heart of successful rituals is an understanding among everyone involved about what will be happening and what they should be doing during the events. Do you know what it's like to attend a religious service and not know whether to sit, stand, or kneel, and where the hymns can be found? No matter how beautiful or meaningful the ceremony, you feel uncomfortable. For people attending wedding events, it's the same thing. If they know what to do along the way, they can settle into the experience and enjoy themselves. If they feel uncertain, they likely will feel anxious and disconnected from your wedding.

Let's start with a wedding where many guests felt out of the loop. Phil and Terri faced a scheduling challenge when they made their wedding plans. They could only get their favorite church at noon and their preferred reception facility at 5 p.m. This meant a gap of more than four hours. The close family and the wedding party were prepared to fill the time (lunch, followed by relaxing at the reception hotel where they had booked rooms), but the other guests were on their own. As people milled around after the ceremony, guests asked each other what they planned to do. Those who lived close to the church said they thought they would go home, have lunch, and do local errands (probably changing clothes twice). Those who were not from the neighborhood inquired of locals where they might find lunch and a mall to shop for the next four hours. In the meantime, the wedding party and immediate family left to do their thing.

The confusion continued. Many guests arrived at the reception before the parents and the wedding party showed up. People asked one another if anyone had spotted the bridal couple yet, and if there was going to be a reception line to greet them. No one knew, but people promised to pass the word once they found out. The bar presented another confusing situation. When it opened, it was not clear whether it was a cash bar or an open bar. Guests had to ask the bartender and then scramble for exact change because he had a limited cash drawer. By the time the well-rested bridal party arrived (some had gone swimming in the hotel pool), the guests were tense. A cocktail reception followed, with no reception line, and with the guests wondering how soon before they could eat; there were only light hors d'oeuvres and some had skipped lunch. Our point here is that only the insiders know what to expect, and the rest were out of the loop. The reception was flat. Lesson: *If you want people to feel comfortable and connected to your wedding, anticipate their needs and let them know what is going on.*

Here's a wedding where the planners knew how to take care of guests. A couple of weeks before the wedding, the mother of the bride sent out of town guests a map of the area and a schedule of events. She also informed them politely that, because so many guests were flying in, they were on their own to get from the airport to the hotel, via cab or car rental, but she sent detailed directions to the hotel. In their rooms when they arrived at their hotel was a schedule of events and detailed directions from the hotel to the groom's dinner and the church, along with tourist bureau information about local restaurants, malls, and museums for those planning to stay longer.

Having been confused guests at other weddings, the bridal couple and the bride's parents also wanted everyone to know what to expect during the evening of the wedding. At the bottom of the order of service they put a notice that the bride and groom would greet the guests at the reception after the photos, rather than immediately after the ceremony. Guests were invited to proceed to the reception for drinks and hors d'oeuvres prior to the arrival of the wedding party. At each seat at the reception was an order of events for the reception itself: arrival of the wedding party, opening prayer, toasts, buffet line, cutting of the cake, and dancing. There was also an estimated time when the bride and groom would depart, something that many guests like to know so that they can plan how long to stay if they want to see the bridal couple off.

The planners of this wedding also put a lot of thought into the seating assignments at the reception, putting together people who knew one another, and when that was not completely possible, combining people who had something in common, for example, a similar occupation or hailing from the same part of the country. They also took into account who was sociable or shy.

This may sound like a lot of organizing, and more than you want to bother with, but mostly it was just informing all guests of what the planners already know, and thinking about ways to connect people informally. Everyone at this wedding knew what to expect and how to get where they need to be. They felt well cared for. The result was a high level of comfort among out of town and local guests alike, and good mixing between people who did not know one another. When you take good care of your guests, they can share fully in the joy of your wedding, which is the one reason to go through all of the work and stress to have a public wedding.

The days surrounding your wedding are likely to be the most intense ones of your life, right up there with the births of your children, and more sadly, deaths in your family. Births, deaths, and weddings—three events in human life that are too big for just the couple and the immediate family. We bring our clan and friends together at such time and expense, not just because it's expected of us or because we get more gifts that way, but because we sense that this event is bigger than the two of us, and bigger than our inner circle of loved ones. In a sense, you already married each other when you made your promise to be committed for life. The rest makes it public and official. In some ways the wedding may be more important for those who share it with you, because it helps them realize that you are now in their lives as a couple, no longer just as individuals. On a more personal level, weddings help guests reflect on what marriage has meant to them in their own lives. When Bill was asked to give brief remarks during the wedding ceremony of friends in 1983, he reflected on what a wedding can mean to those who come to celebrate and bear witness. This is what he said:

> I want to speak today to everyone except the bride and groom, because they have been reflecting on their own about the meaning and importance of this event. Instead I want to speak to the rest of us, because I think we all bring marriages with us into this place. We bring our parents' and grandparents' marriages. We are the living products of their unions. What we have learned in life about love and anger and closeness and fairness and sexuality, we have learned in large measure from them. So we carry our parents' and grandparents' marriages around in our bodies and our minds. They are with us today in this place.
>
> If we have never been married, we still bring a personal marriage here. We bring a marriage of our fantasies, a marriage that we might want to have in the future, or maybe have decided not to have. As we look at this new marriage beginning, we think about what we might want out of a marriage, and what we want to avoid. We say to ourselves, when we observe other

couples present here: "I would never act like that if I were married," or "I would never put up with that," or "This is what I would want if I were married." And so we dream of our ideal mate.

If we are divorced or widowed, we bring here today the marriage of our past and possible marriage of our future. We remember our own wedding day, a beginning that we hoped would not end this way or so soon, but did. We regret what was bad about the marriage or how it ended, but we try to concentrate on celebrating what was good. If we've been through a divorce, we may be inspired by the hope this wedding represents, and hope that enduring, loving unions are indeed possible in a fragile world.

If we come as married people, particularly if we are happily married, we renew our marriage here today. We remember our decision to marry, and whether it was a tortuous decision or an easy one. We remember our wedding day, how we felt, how our lover looked, who was with us then and is still with us, and who has passed from our lives. We remember the little things that went wrong, as when I said "With this wing, I thee wed." We remember the enthusiasm we began our marriage with, our vast hope for the future, our certain sense of being a special couple unlike any other. We remember that day as the beginning of the exquisite and perilous adventure our marriage has been.

My message to you today is that this wedding only appears to be just for this couple who brought us together. It is really their gift to us.